DARTMOOR FOREST

C000069102

A Social History from Enclosure to Abandonment

DARTMOOR FOREST FARMS

A Social History from Enclosure to Abandonment

— *Elisabeth Stanbrook* —

DEVON
BOOKS

First published in Great Britain in 1994 by Devon Books

Copyright © 1994 Elisabeth Stanbrook

*All rights reserved. No part of this publication
may be reproduced, stored in a retrieval system,
or transmitted in any form or by any means without
the prior permission of the copyright holder.*

British Library Cataloguing in Publication Data

Data for this publication is available from the British Library

ISBN 0 86114 887 8

DEVON BOOKS
OFFICIAL PUBLISHER TO DEVON COUNTY COUNCIL

Halsgrove House
Lower Moor Way
Tiverton
Devon EX16 6SS

Telephone: 01884 243242
Facsimile: 01884 243325

Printed in Great Britain by
Longdunn Press, Bristol

CONTENTS

ACKNOWLEDGEMENTS

I am indebted to the various archives, libraries and record offices whose staff made available to me the relevant documents I needed to consult. I would therefore like to thank the Duchy of Cornwall Offices of London, Bradninch (now closed) and Princetown; Devon Record Office, Exeter; West Devon Record Office, Plymouth; West Country Studies Library, Exeter; Plymouth City Library; The British Library, London; The Newspaper Library, Colindale; Public Record Office (Chancery Lane and Kew), and Somerset House, London.

I am also indebted to Dr Tom Greeves and Mr John Somers Cocks for reading through these chapters and giving me both valuable advice and encouragement. Again, I am grateful to Dr Greeves, and also to my parents, for accompanying me out to the various sites and helping with the fieldwork.

My thanks also go to the many people who willingly gave their time to talk to me about their memories or to share their knowledge with me:

Mr George Allen, Rev. M. Bateman, Rev. Baycock, Rev. N. Bliss, Mr D. Brunsden, Rev. Bulley, Dr Michael Caton, Mr Arthur Clarke, Mr & Mrs Roy Chorley, Mrs Diana Coaker, Mrs Rosalind Cronin, Dr J. Daly, Mrs W. Daymond, Mrs Judith Farmer, Cdr H. Fox, Mr David German, Mr Eddie Hain, Mr Charles Hankin, Rev. P. Harrison, Dr Graham Haslam, Miss Betty Hawker, Mr John Haynes, Mr J. Hunt, Mr Tom Hutchings, Mr John King, Miss Elizabeth Knowling, Mrs Margaret Lawrence, Mr Brian Le Messurier, Dr E. Lunt, Mrs A.A. Matthews, Mr Jack O'Hara, Mr Tony Owen-Evans, Mr Martin Perryman, Mrs Diana Phillpotts, Mrs Dorothy Richards, Mrs Jennifer Robertson, Mr G.D. Rouse, Mrs H. Saunders, Mrs Margaret Steemson, Mrs G. Stone, Mr Norman Stone, Mr Colin Sturmer, Mr E.A. Wade, Mr Richard Waller, Mr Bernard Walsh, Mr & Mrs Percy Waye, Mr Wonnacott.

The author and publisher gratefully acknowledge the support of the Dartmoor National Park Authority in bringing this work to publication.

PLATE ACKNOWLEDGEMENTS

Teignhead and Manga Farms: *page 12*, Devon County Council, Westcountry Studies Library, ref. E/C/952; *page 19*, The British Museum; *page 29*, Lady Sayer and Mr Brian Le Messurier; *page 31*, Mr Martin Perryman; *page 33*, Mrs Grace Landon; *page 34*, Mr A.H.D. Davies; *page 37*, Dr Tom Greeves.

John Bishop's House: *page 58 (upper)*, Miss Valerie James and Mrs J Sanders; *page 58 (lower)*, Mrs Jane Somers Cocks; *page 59*, copyright © BBC.

Nuns Cross Farm: *page 61*, Mr Ron Cooper; *pages 62 & 63*, Mr David German; *page 64*, Mrs Helen Harris.

The Ockery: *page 73*, Mr Ron Joy; *page 74*, Mr Richard Stanbrook. *Plans: Figs 1, 2 & 3 redrawn by Mr Francis Stanbrook from plans held by the Duchy of Cornwall Office (DCO)/DC/Dartmoor/Box 28.*

Huntingdon Warren: *pages 79 & 95 (left)*, Mr Percy Waye; *page 90*, Mrs Margaret Steemson; *page 91*, Mr Jack O'Hara; *pages 95 (right), 96, 98 & 100*, Dr Tom Greeves; *pages 101 & 103 (left)*, *Herald Express*, Torquay; *page 103 (right)* Mr A.H.D. Davies; Plan: DCO/DC/Dartmoor/Box 17.

Whiteslade or Snaily House: *page 108*, Devon County Council, Westcountry Studies Library; *page 110 (left)*, Mr Alan Pattison; *page 112*, Chapman Collection, Devon Record Office (ref. DRO 1578).

All other photographs are by the author or from the author's collection.

Front cover: John Hooper outside the original Nuns Cross Farm. Courtesy Ron Cooper.

Back cover: Carrie Waye with daughter Stella at Huntingdon Warren. Courtesy Tom Greeves.

LIST OF ABBREVIATIONS

DCNQ: *Devon & Cornwall Notes & Queries*
DCO (B) (L) (P): Duchy of Cornwall Office, Bradninch, London or Princetown
DNP: Dartmoor National Park
DRO (Exeter): Devon Record Office, Exeter
LTA: Land Tax Assessment
PRO: Public Record Office
RCHME: Royal Commission on the Historical Monuments of England
TDA: *Transactions of the Devonshire Association*
WDRO (Plymouth): West Devon Record Office, Plymouth

INTRODUCTION

It was my interest in the story of Snaily House on the East Dart and the finding of discrepancies between its folklore and documentation that led to this research. I found unravelling the social history fascinating and through this I became interested in other well known ruined dwellings too. This undertaking has given me several years of absorbing work. I found much of what had been written was inaccurate, and that some of these inaccuracies, written at the turn of the century, can be attributed to William Crossing. However it must be remembered that many records were not available to him and he had to rely a great deal upon oral information. Although an extremely valuable source of information, oral history, as with any other, is never completely reliable. Census returns, again, are invaluable but not noted for their infallibility; for example, people were either reluctant to give their ages or they simply did not know them. The 1841 census recorded ages in 5 year bands for those aged over 14, so this produced inaccuracies. Wrong information was sometimes deliberately given to an enumerator; for example, the illegitimate child of a daughter would be recorded as the child of the daughter's parents.

I have researched the histories of nine farms in all, one of which, Manga Farm, is included in the chapter on Teignhead Farm. Huntingdon Warren was a rabbit farm, and some of the others such as The Ockery and John Bishop's House were only very small holdings, with the occupiers often working elsewhere as well. Dating the actual building of these farms was very difficult and sometimes impossible as it was never recorded, but by careful study of various documents, maps and leases, an approximate date could often be estimated. By coincidence rather than design, all the farms were on Duchy of Cornwall land.

Since 1337, the Forest of Dartmoor has been the property of each successive Duke of Cornwall. The history of this has been well documented in a number of publications which include discussions on the forming of the ancient tenements. Excellent accounts can be found in *The Duchy of Cornwall* and *Dartmoor — A New Study* (see references at end of Introduction). I will touch upon it briefly.

The occupiers of each ancient tenement had a copyhold of inheritance, recorded in the Lydford Manor Court Rolls, and could bequeath the farm in their wills or sell it. They paid a small rent and enjoyed turbary and pasturage rights on the Forest lands. In return, they had to attend the Forest Courts held at Lydford Castle and help in the Forest Drifts. An heir or new tenant had the right to enclose an extra parcel of eight acres of land, known as a newtake. This right was frequently abused and a much larger acreage was often enclosed, the excuse being that bog and rock comprised a large part of the land. Thus over the years, much open moorland was claimed by holders of the ancient tenements, and so passed out of Duchy control. This caused the Duchy considerable consternation and in 1796 they banned this old system of acquiring newtakes.[1]

Large tracts of land had also been removed from Duchy control by 'improvers'. By the late 1700s, Britain was entering the agricultural revolution which was to change the face of farming. The growth in population due to a decline in the death-rate as a result of better public hygiene and medical science, led to an increase in the demand for food, which in turn led to more land needed for farming. A high return required for every acre resulted in the demand for new farming methods. These included the planting of clover and root crops to cleanse the soil instead of leaving the land to lie fallow for a year. Cattle could also be fed on these crops during the winter months instead of being slaughtered and salted down for human consumption. Thus the supply of fresh meat became available all the year round. As well as new crops, new methods came to the fore with experiments in stock breeding, manure, drainage and tillage. At first, these agricultural innovations were undertaken by those with capital who could carry the loss should they fail; the smaller farmer was not able to take the financial risk.

It was this interest in agricultural pursuits amongst wealthy individuals that resulted in vast areas of moorland being enclosed; for example, by Mr (later to become Sir) Thomas Tyrwhitt, Mr Judge Buller and Messrs Crawford and Fleming. In fact, it was Buller who, together with Mr Charles Hole, put forward the notion of enclosing the whole of the Forest of Dartmoor and, within it, forming a new parish. It was argued that the Duchy land was boggy, unprofitable, uninhabited and far from the parish church. It would be more profitable to enclose, drain and, where possible, cultivate it.[2]

As set out in the Petition of 1791, this new parish was to be called 'St George' and the bounds would be as follows (the spellings are those given in the Petition):

from Wallabrook Head to the Heath Stone, to Assicombe Barrow to Whitton Torr to Dart Bow to Bear Down Torr to Broad Hole to Blackabrook Bridge on the Turnpike Road leading to Tavistock to the Boundary Stone at or near Jobbers Causeway to South Hessary Torr to Sywards Cross to Eylesborough to Plymhead to Ermeshead to Redlake Foot to East Whiteaborough to West Wallabrook to Knattahill to Knatteford to Dryfield Ford (otherwise Crefield Ford) to Drylake (otherwise Dryworks) to Wobrook Foot whence it falls into the West Dart to East Dart and by the said East Dart to Wallabrook to Wallebrook Head.

Leases would be granted as thought suitable. On the death of a customary tenant, the new or succeeding tenant would be able to take a newtake, to be set out and allocated by the Land Reeve and the customary freeholder. Those areas not enclosed under the Act would be deemed waste and barren lands. For the tenant, there would still be turbary rights and the depasturing of cattle.

Land to the value of £1200 was to be sold to pay for the building of a church and parsonage, and the advowson was to be invested in all future Dukes of Cornwall. The first Rector of the parish was to have been Christopher Cunningham Vickery, clerk to the then Rector of Lydford. However, three years later, it was decided the Rector would be William Feorward Nickell. A resident curate would also be appointed. All tithes were to be paid to the new Rector rather than to the incumbents of Lydford or Widecombe.

New roads were to be laid over the parish with a width of 30 feet (9.1m) between the fences. Various Parish Officers were to be appointed; Constables, Overseers of the Poor, Churchwardens and a Surveyor of the Highways.

The Petition was signed in 1791 by several of the customary tenants; Charles Hole, Justice Buller, James Templer, Thomas Leaman. R. Nosworthy, John Leaman, John French, Elias Babbacombe, George Tapper, John Willcocks, Richard Wills, William Norrish, Rick Stranger, Philip Michelmore, John Woodley, Philip Angel, James Hamlyn and Joseph Sanders.[3]

Not all Duchy tenants wanted this enclosure to take place, notably the smaller farmers. It was also opposed by some Duchy officials such as Richard Gray, who was the Deputy Auditor and Clerk of the Prince's Council and also the Deputy Surveyor-General to the Duchy, and William Simpson who was the Duchy's Land Surveyor. They were concerned that "The Duchy Yoke" would be thrown off, and that the rights of the venville men and the peat cutters would be ignored.[4] After much debate, the Bill did not go through and the parish of St George was never formed.

The moor continued to be enclosed but the Prince's Council decided to make tenants more accountable "by granting a series of leases mainly in the first decade of the nineteenth century."[5]

Many of these farms did not survive; Dartmoor's terrain and climate not being suited to intensive agriculture as the lessees and sub-tenants often found to their cost. Farms like those of Fox Tor and Whiteslade were only worked for about sixty years, while that of Brown's House had an even shorter life-span.

Frequent references to Mr Charles Barrington are made throughout this book; he was the Duchy of Cornwall's Steward and High Bailiff of Dartmoor. Initially he lived at Brimpts and then he moved to Tor Royal at Princetown, the one-time home of Sir Thomas Tyrwhitt. Barrington is described by Crossing as "Urbane and kind of heart"[6] and it seems he was greatly respected by the Duchy tenants.

In essence, this publication is not about farming techniques or the running of the Duchy estate; this has been done by people far better qualified. Instead, it is intended as a tribute to those people who lived and worked in these often isolated moorland dwellings. They had to endure some extremely difficult conditions: overcrowding, poverty, endless repairing of their homes and outbuildings, the unyielding terrain and the appalling weather which Dartmoor can produce throughout all seasons. These were conditions under which most people today would not be prepared to live.

During the course of researching the histories of these farms, it was tempting to get side-tracked and explore avenues not directly relevant. Some of these irrelevances have crept in as I felt them to be of sufficient interest, and I hope readers will bear with me when they come across them.

I experienced certain difficulties when I came to researching those farms that had survived into the twentieth century. Little has been recorded and local memory tends to be at odds with the rare piece of documentation available. As time progresses, more records will become available, but in the meantime, I would be delighted to hear from anyone, at my publishers' address, with memories and photographs (of which there seems to be a dearth) of Dartmoor farms, not only those included in this book, but others too, as I shall be continuing my researches. I feel it is important to record the history of these places and the people who lived in them, before it passes from living memory and they are forgotten.

Elisabeth Stanbrook
July 1994

REFERENCES

1. Harris, H. "Dartmoor" in Gill, C. (Ed.) *The Duchy of Cornwall.* David & Charles 1987 p.108
2. DCO(L) Enclosure Bill Book 1797
3. loc. cit.
4. Somers Cocks, J. "Exploitation" in Gill, C. (Ed.) *Dartmoor: A New Study.* David & Charles 1970 p.249
5. Haslam, G. "Evolution" in Gill, C. (Ed.) *The Duchy of Cornwall* David & Charles 1987 p.46
6. Crossing, C. *One Hundred Years on Dartmoor* Devon Books 1987 p.86

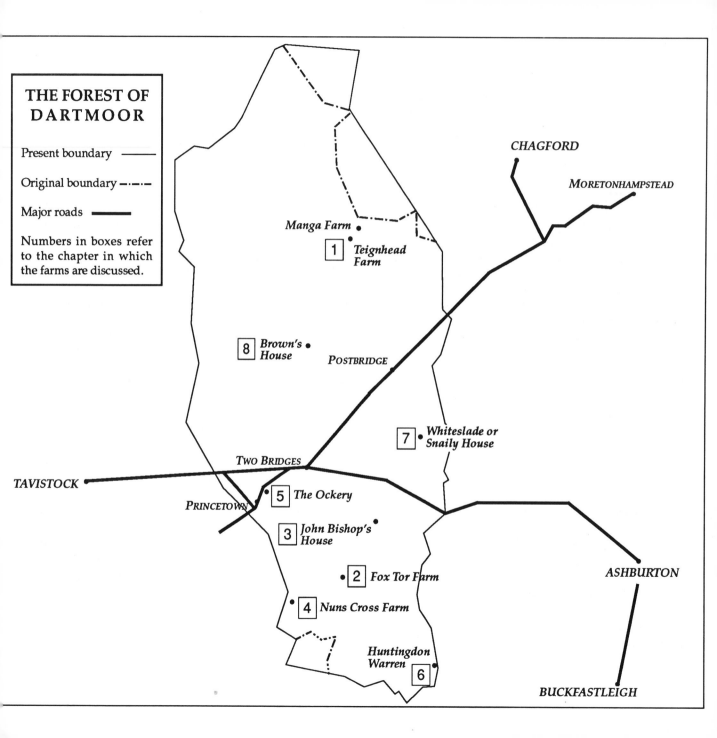

THE FOREST OF
DARTMOOR

Present boundary ———

Original boundary —··—··—

Major roads ▬▬▬▬

Numbers in boxes refer
to the chapter in which
the farms are discussed.

CHAGFORD

MORETONHAMPSTEAD

Manga Farm

[1] Teignhead
Farm

[8] Brown's
House

POSTBRIDGE

[7] Whiteslade or
Snaily House

TWO BRIDGES

TAVISTOCK

[5] The Ockery

PRINCETOWN

[3] John Bishop's
House

[2] Fox Tor Farm

ASHBURTON

[4] Nuns Cross Farm

Huntingdon
Warren

[6]

BUCKFASTLEIGH

1. TEIGNHEAD AND MANGA FARMS
The building of the farms 1808 - 1817

The most popular misconceptions about Teignhead Farm are that it was built in 1780, enlarged in 1808, and was pre-dated by the smaller Manga Farm. William Crossing was undoubtedly responsible for much of this, but it must be remembered that his main sources of information were oral and not documentary. His references to dates and occupiers of the farms have subsequently been repeated over the years by many who have written about Dartmoor. No substantial new information has been forthcoming other than what has appeared in Eric Hemery's *High Dartmoor* (1983). Detailed information about Manga Farm is difficult to find, probably because Teignhead Farm was the larger of the two and was occupied to a far greater extent. Manga farmhouse appears to have been frequently used for storage purposes.

This chapter, based on several years research, gives a greater insight into two of Dartmoor's most remote farmsteads. Teignhead farmhouse can be found at SX 635 843 while Manga farmhouse is at SX 639 848. Both are situated at a height of 1475 feet (450m) above sea level.

In 1805, Mr Matthew Crawford arrived on Dartmoor from the county of Longaford in Ireland and made two unsuccessful attempts to lease land from the Duchy of Cornwall. The first land of his choice had a prior claim by John Hussey Esq., while the second, north of Postbridge, had been leased to the Hullett brothers.[1] They had taken over a lease formerly in the possession of Mr Paterson. Having been twice disappointed, Crawford joined forces with Lt. Col. Richard Fleming from Wandsworth, Surrey, and in 1808, their application to lease land from the Duchy met with success.

The parcel of land concerned comprised 1551 acres and was situated towards the eastern boundary of the Forest of Dartmoor. The actual bounds of the enclosure were North upon "Hey Down", North East and East upon "Ruther Lake, Gidley Common and Chagford Common", South upon Sir John Davie's enclosure of Fernworthy, South West and West upon "Sittaford Hill and Great Varracomb" and North West upon "Watern Hill".[2] "Hey Down" refers to Heydon or Headon, the hill between the Wallabrook and Gallaven Brook. "Ruther Lake" refers to Rue Lake.

Crawford and Fleming undertook to "inclose and improve the same and erect thereon two substantial houses with suitable outbuildings for the purpose of establishing two separate farms";[3] in other words, the farms of Teignhead and Manga. The lease was granted for a period of 99 years from 1808 at a rent of £58.3s.11d, although this was later reduced because only 904 acres were actually enclosed. There was a proviso that the two farms must be erected within ten years from the date of the lease.

Crossing sited Manga Farm (to which he refers as "Mandles") on Great Varracombe,[4] and it has since been claimed he did this in error.[5] This claim may

"Teign Head in Dartmoor" by Duncan after J. Strutt. c.1828.

have been made because the modern O.S. maps attribute the names of Great and Little Varracombe to two brooks running into the North Teign river, but it is conceivable that Crossing was not mistaken. The lease map for the farms offers no name for either brook. Instead, Little Varracombe is shown as a tract of land to the south of Manga Brook, while Great Varracombe is shown as the land to the north of the brook, with its western fringes abutting the eastern flank of Whitehorse Hill. This is the area where Manga Farm was to be built. This was also known as Manga Hill. Hemery places Great Varracombe at Quinter's Man, citing the bounds given on the lease as documentary evidence. But it seems he only saw mention of three bounds, ie. "Sittaford Tor, Watern Hill and Great Varracombe", thus misinterpreting their topographical location. At no time is Quinter's Man referred to in either the lease or on the lease map. Initially, Manga Farm was called Varracombe[6] and, at some time after 1829, became known by its familiar name, although it was often documented in records as Teignhead or Teign Farm due to its being a part of the Teignhead enclosures. "Manga" was undoubtedly adopted for the farm because of its close proximity to Manga Rock, Manga Brook, Manga Hole and Manga Ford. (The name Manga Brook conflicts with Hemery's claim that it was known as Great Mire Stream and renamed by the inhabitants of the farm. But the latter may well have been an alternative name).

A further piece of evidence to support Crossing is a letter dated 1852,[7] (see below p.22). It states quite clearly that the Teignhead enclosures were known locally as "Varicombe". So was Crossing really at fault, or was he merely using the topographical terms of his time, or even quoting those of an older generation from whom he gathered much of his information?

The Indenture for Crawford's and Fleming's land was signed and dated 13th May 1808. It has been suggested that this was drawn up to create additional enclosures, on the assumption that Teignhead Farm was built in 1780,[8] but a Duchy map of c.1802-4 clearly shows that no enclosures had ever been built in this area[9] as does the O.S. Surveyors Drawing of the area in 1802-3. The Duchy's 1786 Survey which listed all newtakes in the Forest of Dartmoor had no reference to a newtake at Teignhead either.[10]

That no enclosures or farms existed here before 1808 is further substantiated in a document of 1842.[11] It has already been mentioned that the land finally enclosed was 904 acres. The construction of the enclosure walls resulted in a dispute between the wall builders and the Gidleigh commoners who felt that encroachments were being made upon their common land. Maps held by the Duchy laying out the bounds of the parish of Lydford were based upon mis-information given to them by the Rev. James Holman Mason, who was the Deputy Rider of the Forest as well as Vicar of Widecombe. In 1842, the Tithe Commission ordered an investigation into the parish boundaries and the dispute of 1808, and the documentation of the Inquiry is most informative.

Having secured their lease, Crawford and Fleming employed the services of Mr William Rogers as their Agent, and he too came over from Ireland in 1808, staying initially at Fernworthy. Giving evidence of what happened to the Inquiry, Rogers told the Commission, "I came on the moor in 1808 from Ireland to superintend an enclosure marked by Crawford. When I came first, there was no wall on the common. I was the manager of the enclosure. I superintended the makers of the newtake. It is known as the newtake."[12]

At the 1842 Inquiry, Rogers gave his age as "about" 60, and so was therefore born c.1782. This would have made it impossible for him to have built the Teignhead Farm in 1780.

The statements made by local people in 1842 give an indication of the ill feeling towards the enclosures. A Gidleigh man, Mr Tucker, stated that "I saw a hedge erecting to inclose Squire Crawford's newtake. If the hedge had been completed, it would have taken 700 or 800 acres from Gidley Common. ... I saw the hedge dug down. It was dug down on the day we perambulated the Bounds of Gidleigh. ... William Rogers, the Agent of Mr Crawford was on the spot at the time."[13] This was confirmed by Rogers in his statement that "118 yards or perch of the wall had been erected. Then the Gidley people came out - a great number ... I dare say 100 - this was in 1808. They pulled down a great part of the fence. I saw it done. ... We never rebuilt the fence torn down. We built another fence."[14]

This other fence or stone wall was threatened with the same fate by the Gidleigh commoners, but as it did not encroach as much on to their common land, they reconsidered. The Tithe Commission finally decided to adopt the bounds given by the people of Gidleigh, thus the dividing line between the two parishes crosses part of the northern area of Teignhead newtake. A more detailed account of this dispute has been covered in an excellent article by John Somers Cocks.[15]

One of Rogers' workmen was Mr Westcott who "when a boy helped to build it, and his father 'ripped the stones for it'".[16]

Some of the stones employed came from the Blacksmith's Shop, a tinners' mill on the west bank of the North Teign. Part of a mouldstone can be seen in the walling near the site. There is also what appears to be a tinners' mouldstone in the ruins of Teignhead Farm outhouse, which would have made a useful drinking trough for the livestock and, given its size,

Trough in the cattle shed at Teignhead Farm.

Teignhead clapper bridge.

would have been enlarged for the purpose. However, it has been suggested that its origin as a tinners' mouldstone is doubtful.[17]

Rogers was also responsible for the construction of Teignhead clapper bridge and the stones for it are supposed to have been sledged down a snow-covered Manga Hill to the river below.[18] This bridge was dislodged in 1826 when the North Teign became very swollen, and it had to be re-built. Feather and tare marks in the stones are in evidence.

The smaller clapper just down river may also have suffered the same fate as the larger one in 1826. This was not restored until 1990 in memory of F. H. (Harry) Starkey who, together with a friend, discovered it lying in the river bed. Feather and tare

marks on it suggest it may be contemporary with the Teignhead clapper, and built for access to Manga Farm although there are no gateways (or walled up ones) in the extensive stone walling with which one is confronted upon crossing from the east to the west bank. The hill up to Manga Farm is also steep from this point.

At the northern end of the newtake where the wall spans the North Teign, upright granite pillars were erected in the river on which timber poles were supported. This prevented the livestock from wandering off onto the moor. This area is known as Rails. Timber is no longer found here. For a long time, barbed wire was used in its place, but in 1991 this was replaced with iron rails.

Little is known of Rogers himself, but a resident of Chagford (whose late husband was a descendant) provided information about his Irish background. At the close of the eighteenth century, Ireland was suffering a potato famine which gave rise to frequent rioting. In 1802, Rogers was involved with one of these rebellions and had the command of a detachment, the Kenagh Light Infantry. They were sent to defend the passage at Lanesborough on the River Shannon.

When Rogers came over to Dartmoor six years later, he lived at Fernworthy until Teignhead Farm was built, after which he moved into the new farmhouse. In his statement of 1842, he disclosed that "I had the care of the place 20 years and my residence was there most of the time".

However the Land Tax Assessment lists (LTA's) show that he resided at Teignhead Farm until 1818 and then moved to Fernworthy shortly before his marriage to Ann Endacott who had presented him with a son, Henry, the year before.[19] From the end of 1818 to 1822, he rented Gidleigh Barton, before moving back to Fernworthy until about 1829. So although he had "the care of the place", his actual residence at Teignhead seems to have been only until 1818.

Oddly, Hemery refers to Rogers as appearing in the LTA's for 1798, "chargeable for Fernworthy". But on checking this reference, I found that it was leased from the Duchy to Sir John Davie and occupied by Mr John Brown. In any case, Rogers was still in Ireland.

Since 1811, the Rev. J.H. Mason had been the Deputy Rider "in possession of the Agistment of the whole Forest at a rent of £40"[20] per annum. In 1817, whilst living at Teignhead Farm, Rogers rented from Mason what he thought was a small part of the North quarter of the Forest, between Stone Tor Hill and Shovel Down, which he then sub-let to Mr Hannaford and Mr Waldron, together with part of the newtake. The renting of this land from Mason was short-lived as it did not lie within the Duchy bounds and was therefore erroneously leased to him. The impounding of commoners' cattle at Dunnabridge pound had met with protestations from injured parties, and Mason was compelled to reimburse Rogers the £2 rent that he had taken two months previously.[21] Hannaford and Waldron retained the newtake and, as Rogers himself was living at Teignhead Farm, they would have occupied Manga Farm. While at Teignhead, Rogers farmed bullocks, making a profit for Mr Crawford.[22] In 1828, Rogers' wife Ann died, as did a two-year-old daughter, Catherine. He later moved to Shapley and then to Torr in Chagford, and in 1842, he was living at Forder in North Bovey.[23]

Accommodation in the thatched Teignhead farmhouse comprised a kitchen, parlour, dairy and three bedrooms.[24] A cattlehouse stood to the north of the farm, while an attached outhouse or linhay was on the southern end. The ruins of the barn, situated away from the house, virtually opposite the sheep dip, do not appear on the 1840 Tithe Map. Nor does the barn appear in the aquatint by Duncan c.1828, (originally drawn by J. Strutt) so it was probably built c.1840s, and was only to last a few decades as it had gone by the early 1900s.

Manga farmhouse was thatched and single storey, built into the side of Manga Hill which was dug out to accommodate it. It had three rooms; the southern-most one was the kitchen and a large fireplace occupied the north wall, still discernible through the rubble that now fills the interior. The entrance to the porch gave access to the central room, so it can be assumed that the northernmost room was the bedroom. Outside, there was an attached turf house on the southern wall, a cowshed to the north where a

The sheep dip at Teignhead Farm.

drainage channel is still in evidence, and an outhouse to the east.

It is from the Tithe Map that we are given some idea of the layout of the fields surrounding the farms during this period. Teignhead Farm had nine enclosed fields. Of these, two to the east of the house were meadow, the plot to the south where the trees grew until recently was pasture, the northern two of the three fields to the west of the house were arable. The large southernmost field was 'coarse', while the others were unspecified, except the small enclosed parcel of land immediately outside the front of the house which was the garden.

There are some interesting gateposts at Teignhead - notably of the "slot and L" type, discussed by Worth. He was of the opinion that none of the gateposts of this type had been made since 1800 "and that most are much older".[25] This would suggest that those at Teignhead came from Fernworthy Farm, with which William Rogers had a close association. Indeed, as Worth says, this type of gatepost can still be seen in the old stone walling at Fernworthy. Another gatepost at Teignhead, situated behind the linhay, is a granite roller, although at the time of writing, it has fallen down. These were in general use "for rolling wheat and pasture grounds".[26]

Manga Farm was completely self-contained and had three enclosures. The track from Teignhead clapper to the farm passed through a stroll between the two southernmost fields, the eastern one listed as arable. Hemery maintains plough marks are visible here, but this is questionable. The large north enclosure was listed as 'coarse'. Piles of stones resulting from field clearances can still be seen. Opposite the farmhouse was an enclosed parcel of land which was the garden, as at the larger farm, but this was defined as such in a later document of 1844, detailed below. At the back of the farmhouse and cowshed was a small farmyard.

The water supplies to the farms came from potwater leats cut from Manga Brook. The Teignhead leat came around the hill above the farm to the walled enclosure once planted with trees, where it was channelled down the hill and round to the courtyard. It is difficult to trace it in its latter stage, but it seems that it entered a small reservoir just in front of where a corrugated iron shed now stands. The sheep dip was fed by a leat taken off this main leat at a strategic point on the hill above. Excess water drained away on the other side of the track.

The Manga Farm leat passed around Manga Hill, through a gate in the wall above the house and downhill to a small reservoir at the front of the house where the water ran into a granite water shute. A trough can be found here. Excess water drained away down a channel on the eastern side of the hill.

Two etchings by Samuel Prout may provide us with the earliest record of what the farms looked like before 1819. One is captioned 'Teign Head Farm' in the publication *The New Drawing Book* and dated 1st January 1819[27], while both of them are captioned 'Teignhead Farm' in *A History of Chagford*. If the caption of the other one is correctly attributed, the single storey cottage, although captioned Teign Head Farm, would have been Manga Farm, while the other would be Teignhead. It is fairly safe to assume they were both drawn by 1819 because, as Baring-Gould says, "Prout's work is divided into two clearly defined periods. In the first he drew only English scenes. In 1819 he made his first tour of the Continent, and thenceforth devoted himself almost entirely to foreign subjects".[28]

Trough at Manga Farm.

Reputed to be Teignhead Farm, c.1818, by Samuel Prout.

An etching, possibly of Manga Farm, c.1818, by Samuel Prout.

19

The Tenants 1817 - 1849

It was in December 1817 that Crawford and Fleming sold the lease for the Teignhead enclosures to a gentleman called Mr Plowden Presland, from Middlesex.[29] It is likely that Rogers gave notice to quit the farm at Lady Day in 1818. Presland's financial acumen was not as acute as he might have wished and by 1819 he found himself in debt to Mr Johnathan Henry Key for the sum of £3000. Unable to settle this debt, Presland made over the farms to Key in trust, to secure the debt. The Indenture to that effect was signed in the October of that year.[30] During Key's possession of the lease, Hannaford moved away and was replaced by William Hutchings, whom most likely lived at Manga Farm, Waldron moving across to Teignhead Farm. A descendant of Hutchings told the author that his family occupied Manga farmhouse at an early date in its history, and that a bronze pestle in his possession had always been handed down from father to eldest son since William Hutchings' occupation of the farm.

On the whole, it has proved difficult to obtain detailed information about Teignhead and Manga farms and their occupants before the late 1840s. In fact, in 1844, Gardiner, who was Secretary to the Duchy Council, complained that the lease on the farm had changed hands many times without a properly kept record of lessees.[31] He thus recommended repossession of the farms. Fortunately, searches through parish registers, the 1841 census returns and the Tithe Apportionment provided some information. Between 1825 and 1833, William Hutchings and his wife Mary produced at least four children while living at Manga Farm. Parish registers show that in 1833, an Elizabeth Knapman was living with them and her illegitimate daughter, Grace, was baptised at the same

ceremony as the infant George Hutchings. The small farmhouse must have been very cramped, although there may have been sleeping accommodation under the roof.

In c.1840, Key relinquished the lease on Teignhead newtake and it passed to Mr Isaac Alexander.[32] The Tithe Apportionment shows William Hutchings and Joseph Waldron were still there, but a year later, the 1841 census returns show that the tenants had changed and William Wilkins, a farrier, was now in residence. Manga farmhouse was uninhabited. Alexander was still the lessee and in 1843, Rev. Mason wrote to the Duchy informing them that a Mr White of Moretonhampstead was willing to pay the rent on Mr Alexander's account.[33]

Mr John Brock then took over the lease on the newtake, together with Holming Beam, in December 1843.[34] The next few months saw a deterioration in the condition of both Teignhead and Manga farmhouses and in October 1844, the Duchy sent their surveyor, Mr Shillibeer (possibly a relation of the early nineteenth century surveyor, Shillibeer, who died in 1827), to the farms to make a report, the contents of which are as follows:

"The Dwelling House of the Farm, namely Teignhead, contains two Kitchens, and three Bedrooms over. There was no one at home - and a padlock on the door. The Thatched Roof appears in a condition to keep these Rooms dry. The House, the breadth of, and adjoining the Dwelling on the south side is partially filled with turf - the west side of the Roof requires thatching. A well built wall for about 20 feet in length, and in line with the Dwelling House at the north end has been rebuilt in front to a given height, but not high enough for a roof to have a loft - the back wall of the length and height of the

front has been repaired. The walls in the same run of what has been the cattle houses, are in a ruinous state - no part of the Roofs are left. A new cart bearing the name John Dodd, also a lighter cart, were under a temporary cart shed. A small stack of hay was in one of the plots and a small plot of potatoes, about a quarter of an acre. There was a pig feeding, two store pigs, and some fowls in the yard - the Gate of which wanted a top hook, and to the six plots around the House there were no gates.

We (Mr Mason being with me) found the other Dwelling House called Manger [sic], consisting of three ground rooms, not occupied, the glass of the windows gone, and the three rooms filled with bundles of Rushes and coarse Sedgy grass, and 2 Bags of Potatoes. The roof is in a tolerable state - well thatched. A Cow Shed at the north end, a continuation of the same Roof, appears to be now in use - the wall of which needs repair. A small Turf House at the south end - the Walls and Roof are in a dilapidated state, as well as another outhouse which has no Roof. There is a small garden with some cabbages in it. The inclosure here, as at the other place have no Gates.

The division Fences of both Farms are in a bad state of repair. The outer Boundary fence including the augmented portion has been repaired as parts have fallen."[35]

Two months after this report was made, Brock received a letter from the Duchy informing him that they were sending a Mr Freeth to re-enter the farm and take possession. This is likely to have been in response to Gardiner's recommendation of repossession mentioned above. Brock was far from pleased because, according to him, his rents were paid and he could see no reason for this action. He requested that re-entry be stayed, which is exactly what did happen - not because of his request but because of deep snow! Re-entry did at last take place in March 1845, by which time Brock had vacated the premises anyway. Since Brock's departure, the key to Teignhead farmhouse had been in possession of John Dodd who then handed it over to Mason. The farm was re-entered by Mason, Simon Moore and Richard Coaker, and it can be assumed the necessary repairs were undertaken.

The lease for Teignhead was then obtained by Rev. Mason who sub-let it to Dodd on a week-to-week basis at a rent of 5s.[36] From the abovementioned report, it would appear that Dodd already had an interest in the farm. Crossing mistakenly dates his occupation of the farm as 1817.

A request for the tenancy of Teignhead Farm was submitted to the Duchy in August 1845, and came from a Mr Crawford. As the original Crawford was now dead, this was possibly a relative. His request was refused on the grounds that his proposed rent was too low and, at the same time, Dodd was given notice to quit by Michaelmas of that year. However, he did not leave and his tenancy was put on a more secure footing, and he lived at the farm for a further four years at an annual rent of £30.

In 1848, a tender was sent to the Duchy from a firm interested in planting Scots pines at Teignhead Farm at £3.8s.0d. an acre.[37] There is no evidence of these trees at Teignhead Farm in photographs taken before the turn of the century, so it is doubtful that they were ever planted.

The farmhouse again fell into a bad state of repair. Rev. Mason wrote to Mr Charles Barrington, the Duchy Steward, in December 1848 saying that Dodd planned to leave the farm at Christmas unless the Duchy undertook to repair it; "after the tempestuous weather on Sunday night last, it quite settles the matter with him."[38] After inspecting the premises himself, Barrington confirmed the necessity of these repairs.

The following year, Dodd decided he would have to leave the farm due to his wife's continual ill health. "She has been very unwell for a long time and has been from home for some time for a change of air and has very much improved her health, but almost immediately after her return home she became quite an invalid and the Doctors state that she cannot live at Teignhead, the air is much too strong for her constitution."[39]

Baring-Gould, writing fifty years later, felt that Teignhead Farm was no place for a woman to live for he said, "it is not for many winters that a woman can endure the isolation and retain her reason."[40]

The Endacotts 1849 - 1876

Dodd's departure in 1849 resulted in two applications for tenancy, one from Mr Edward Hutchings of Belstone and the other from Mr James Endacott of North Hill, Chagford. The former's father had been the previous tenant, William Hutchings, who had displayed a reluctance to pay his rent towards the end of his tenancy.[41] This, together with the fact that Edward Hutchings had no livestock, tipped the balance in favour of James Endacott, who did. Although Barrington wanted to put Teignhead Farm out to tender to try and secure a higher rent, the Duchy were not agreeable and Endacott moved in at an annual rent of £35. Records indicate that Rev. Mason no longer had an interest in the farm and that Endacott was now the lessee. He lived here, in the Teignhead farmhouse with his wife, Mary, and his younger children, William, George and Samuel.

During the course of 1850, a Chagford man, Mr Horlock, repeatedly asked the Duchy for the tenancy of Teignhead Farm. Eventually, Barrington asked James Endacott how he was disposed towards this. His answer is rather enlightening in that it gives us the information that Manga farmhouse was still very much intact and habitable, and it also tells us the acreage. He said that he would be willing to quit the farm the following September 29th,

"on condition of being allowed to occupy rent-free until Lady Day 1851 the detached small farmhouse and newtake containing 20 acres or thereabouts comprised within the boundaries of Teignhead Farm."[42]

The 1851 census returns show that James Endacott did occupy Manga Farm, but living at Teignhead Farm was Joseph Waldron again, implying that Mr Horlock was either refused tenancy or that he stayed only a matter of months.

Another request for tenancy of the farm was submitted to the Duchy the following year by Mr Lewis Way who wanted to breed horses and improve the race on the moor. In his letter of application, he indicated that the Teignhead enclosures were known locally as 'Varicombe', as mentioned above.

James Endacott and his family were reluctant to leave Teignhead and to do so demanded a very large sum of money, described by Barrington as "not thinkable".[43] In the event, Mr Way was refused the tenancy as Endacott was determined to stay, having spent a considerable sum of his own money on repairs to both Teignhead and Manga farmhouses - £2 and £7 respectively - for which he hoped to receive remuneration from the Duchy.[44] Records did not show whether he ever did!

Manga Farm was the home of James and Mary Endacott for several years. The 1857 *Billing's Directory* lists their son William as the farmer at Teignhead Farm, showing that they no longer sub-let it to the Waldrons. The 1861 census returns show that James was still at Manga Farm where he is described as a farmer of 20 acres. Teignhead Farm was listed as unoccupied meaning that William was away at the time of the census. He did in fact stay at the farm until early 1871.

James Endacott died on 3rd June 1870, and Mr William Perryman, the miller at Yeo Farm near Chagford, had been appointed Endacott's trustee. All the household effects and farm stock were to be sold, with the exception of a few items of domestic furniture. An Inventory, given below,[45] drawn up by Perryman, gives an indication not only of the stock being farmed by the family but also the furniture and fittings that must have been so pertinent to any number of rural farmsteads.

Inventory of Goods and Chattels & Farm Stock late the property of Jas Endacott of Teignhead Farm, Lidford [sic] June 9th, 1870.
Died June 3rd, 1870.

	£.	s.	d.
Clock _____ ?		4.	0.
Kitchen Table & Form		4.	0.
Oil case cover		1.	6.
Square Table		6.	
Kitchen chairs (3)		4.	
Book Shelves		0.	
6 Vols books (Sermons)		0.	
2 Brass Candlesticks		3.	
2 Ironing boxes		0.	
Frill iron		0.	
Tin teapot		0.	

	£.	s.	d.
4 Tea cups & saucers			3.
6 Plates willow pattern			3.
2 Dishes			1.
2 Teapots			2.
Water Jug			2.
2 Chimney curtains			1.
2 Bar Crooks			4.
Pair Tongs		1.	0.
Crock & Tea Kettles		1.	0.
Milk Stove [crossed out]			
2 Iron pails		1.	0.

	£.	s.	d.
14 Milk pans			
1 Basket			
Butter weights & 1/2lb stone			
Butter Tub			
Earthernware pan		10.	0.
Oat measure (round basket)			
2 Flower pots & flowers			
2 Basons [sic]			

Old brass pan
Old Breeching
Old Collar   } worth nothing
Old Kieve
Frame of Chair

Reserve

4 post bed & frame for cov.
Mattress
Feather Tie
2 Sheets
1 Blanket
1 Counterpane
1 Bolster
1 Pillow

	£. s. d.
4 Post Bed & Frame for Cov.	1. 0.
Feather Tie	5. 0.
2 Sheets	6.
1 Quilt	2.
1 Bolster	2. 6.
Hamper	
Utensil	
Chest of Drawers	5. 0.
Old Bed	1. 6.
Mattress	0.
Feather Tie	2. 6.
2 Sheets	6.
1 Quilt	0.
Feather Bolster	1. 0.
Small bed	0.
Straw Tie	0.
Old Sheet	0.
Clothes Box	1. 0.
Coffer }	
	£2. 4. 1.
	1. 6.
	£2. 5. 7.
Ladder (23 stalls)	
Empty Cask	
Pig Stock	
Old Form	
2 old carts	5. 0.
1 Horse [crossed out]	
1 Colt [crossed out]	
1 Goose - setting a brood	
3 Geese & 6 chicken	
Cow & Calf	8. 0. 0.
14 Bullocks	90. 0. 0.
Horse	1. 0. 0.
Harness	5. 0.
Colt	4. 0. 0.

At an Auction held at Gidley Barton on Sept 15th 1870 for the sale of the foregoing Cattle etc., the following were the prices realised.

	£ s. d.
15 Bullocks	82. 17. 6.
1 Cart without wheels	16. 6.
1 Horse	1. 7. 0.
1 Colt	1. 10. 0.
Harness	6. 0.
Scuffle	4. 0.
Pair Drays	6. 0.
" Harrows	3. 0.
8 Geese	1. 12. 0.
	£89. 2. 0.
Calf sold to G.H. Endacott	15. 0.
Cart " " S. Collins	10. 0.
	£90. 7. 0.

Although willing to act as trustee for James Endacott's estate, Perryman did not want the responsibility of running Teignhead and Manga farms and instructed the Duchy accordingly. George Endacott then applied for the lease at a half yearly rent of £15. Other applications were received from Mr Landry, Mr Brooshoof and William Hutchings, but it was George's application that was accepted.

George Endacott, sometimes referred to as "Teignhead George", is supposed to have lived at Manga Farm with his very large family.[46] In 1871, he appears in the census as living in Teignhead farmhouse with his widowed mother and brother Samuel. At that time George was 30 and unmarried. He left the farm in 1876 and there is nothing to suggest that during those years, he married and started a family. Living at Manga Farm with his parents and brothers during the 1850s and 1860s may have given rise to this legend.

The repairs needed to Teignhead farmhouse in 1871 were extensive. New floors, window frames and joists were required together with reparation work to the ceilings, doors, cupboards and the thatched roof. Slates on the porch roof also needed replacing. There are no further references to suggest that Manga farmhouse was to be lived in again, and a letter of 1877 implies that it had been uninhabitable for some time.[47] It is this period that marks its final decay into the ruin we see today.

In 1875, George Endacott's rent was in arrears causing Barrington some concern "from what I can learn, Mr Endacott has, for some time past,been leading a very unsteady life and neglecting his business so much that his relations are doubtful if his mind is not affected."[48]

George did eventually pay his rent but a year later, the same problem arose, together with a fast diminishing stock. The decision was taken to send in the bailiffs to procure the rent, but this was called off at the last possible moment due to payment being made by George's relatives. It was during this time, in April 1876, that George was summoned to appear before the magistrates and we learn that "poor old George Endacott was committed to gaol for a month on Monday for being drunk",[49] leaving the farm unattended. So his relatives moved his cattle to Gidleigh. It appears that George did not get much return for his labours at Teignhead, having to find employment on occasions at Teigncombe where his brother Thomas lived.[50]

The Duchy's general disquiet about George's suitability as a tenant culminated in a notice to quit being served on him in September 1876. Absent from the farm at the time, the notice was left with his mother.[51] In the meantime, one of his brothers, Samuel, and his brother-in-law had applied for joint tenancy but, instead, the farm was put out to tender.

There were several applications for the lease. Messrs French and Tuckett offered £45 per annum; Mr Hawkins, £50 p.a.; Mr Gemmell of Bickleigh, £215 p.a. to include Tor Royal enclosures, Fox Tor Farm and Muddilakes; James Endacott of Gidley Barton, £47 p.a. or £50 if the Duchy built him a dairy and bullock-house for the winter; William and George Hutchings of Belstone, £63 p.a.; and Thomas Stephens of Stannon, Postbridge, £58 p.a. There was also a verbal application from Mrs A. Coaker offering £56 p.a. She expressed a concern that Teignhead Farm would merely become used as a newtake for cattle, at a low price which was "too often done".[52] Hemery mentions a tender from a Mr J. Bartlett, but there was no reference to him in the records.

Gemmell, Lamb, Brock and John Hutchings 1876 - 1923

After due consideration and deciding that Mr Samuel Chaffe would probably have no objections to vacating the land at Fox Tor Farm, Mr John Gemmell's application was accepted, with Mr Hawkins as the second choice.[53] Mr Gemmell's interest in the properties was threefold. Firstly, at Tor Royal, he wanted to cultivate rape using lime as a manure; secondly, he wanted to drain the lands, putting them down to grass afterwards, and erect any necessary buildings; thirdly, at Teignhead, after draining the land, he would breed Scottish sheep and, if this was unsuccessful, he would try cattle, "so you need have no fear of the failure of my experiments".[54] Drainage channels can be seen above Teignhead Farm's leat. These may have been dug during Gemmell's occupation. He also planned to generally improve the moorland. It has been suggested that Mr James Lamb was responsible for introducing Scottish Blackface sheep to Dartmoor, [55] but in fact it was Gemmell who did this and it is probably he who had the sheep-dip at the farm made, with the necessary leat taken off the pot water leat. There was no record of sheep being farmed at Teignhead before Gemmell's time.

Gemmell's application for the four properties was formally accepted in December 1876 and his lease commenced on 25th March 1877. In 1878, he was also leasing Joan Ford's Newtake and Hound or Round Hill. Between George Endacott's departure and the signing of Gemmell's lease, a John Hamlyn lived at Teignhead Farm. [56]

Gemmell's occupation of Teignhead Farm was fraught with problems. Although George Endacott no longer leased the farm, he seemed intent on making a nuisance of himself. In April 1877, Gemmell complained to the Duchy that Endacott had been carting away dung from the farm. Letters that followed show that he and his brother William had actually moved back into the farmhouse and were refusing to leave until the law compelled them to. Gemmell had made arrangements to install a shepherd in the farmhouse and was anxious to carry out necessary repairs in time for his arrival in late May, and this could not be done until the farm was vacated. To add insult to injury, Gemmell had employed John Coaker to plant potatoes for the new shepherd, and the Endacott brothers were busying themselves with pulling them up and planting mangolds in their place. They also planned to acquire 50 or 60 bullocks to graze on the land! [57]

Gemmell's patience was finally stretched to its limit, and in a letter to the Duchy asking them for help in the matter, he angrily refers to George, saying "spare him not". [58] In the end, William Perryman was asked to intervene, and George subsequently said he would

think about leaving! Towards the end of May, the farmhouse did at last fall vacant. In the meantime, Gemmell had travelled up to Scotland to fetch 1300 sheep and he returned to Okehampton with them on 27th May from where they were brought to Teignhead. [59]

From the parish registers it can be assumed that the shepherd Gemmell installed at Teignhead was Peter Murray. They show that in July 1878, his and his wife Christina's son, Peter, was baptised at St Gabriel's Chapel, Postbridge.

As had been the case with George Endacott, Gemmell had a reluctance to pay his rent. The first sign of trouble came shortly after the lease was signed, and the non-payment of rent resulted in a warrant being issued to place the matter in the hands of a broker. [60] Gemmell's slowness in paying may have been due to his annoyance at the farm being occupied by the Endacott brothers, and it was eventually paid.

In April 1879, Gemmell decided to sub-let his lands, with the exception of Fox Tor Farm and Joan Ford's Newtake, to Mr James Lamb of Scotland, who had lately been living on Exmoor. The actual agreement was completed on 21st April, and stated that Gemmell would sub-let Teignhead Farm, Tor Royal, Hound or Round Hill and Muddilakes to Lamb for a rent of £450 for 18 years from 15th May. [61]

The following November, Gemmell was again in trouble for rent arrears. The Duchy's Deputy Receiver authorised the distrain of goods and chattels (live and dead stock) at both Teignhead and Fox Tor Farms. In turn, Lamb had not remitted all his rent to Gemmell and owed him £380, stating that he had a counter-claim against Gemmell which cancelled the amount out. [62] No indication of what this counter-claim might be appears in the records, but at some stage he changed his mind, no doubt when Sawdye

Auctioneers of Ashburton were about to enter Teignhead Farm and seize his goods to the value of the rent arrears - they had just paid a fruitful visit to Fox Tor Farm! This action had "astonished" Gemmell who had, only the day before, paid his overdue rent.[63] That Gemmell was in financial difficulties was becoming apparent because, before the auctioneers removed his sheep, he was trying to dispose of Fox Tor Farm with the sheep "thrown in"![64] In June 1880, a bankruptcy notice appeared in a national newspaper stating that Gemmell had gone into voluntary liquidation. In the London Bankruptcy Court, it was disclosed that he had formed a business partnership with a Mr James Foderick, as farmers at Woolwell Farm, Bickleigh, near Plymouth, but that he was now living in Middlesex, "out of business".[65]

Back in Devon, Lamb's next payment of rent to Gemmell was again outstanding. He had apparently led Lamb to understand that Dartmoor farms were like those in Scotland, and he had since discovered that they were not! He had followed Gemmell's example and brought down Scottish Blackface sheep from Scotland on the understanding that they would be of a hardy enough nature. He felt this had not been the case and he had consequently lost over £1000 in sheep deaths, largely caused by moor-sickness.[66] This is a condition brought on by the absence of the trace element cobalt in the soil, which affects the quality of the grass. Feeling he had been badly misled, Lamb was loathe to pay Gemmell and this may have been a contributory factor in his refusal to pay on the previous occasion.

However, no doubt sensing that Gemmell's unfortunate financial situation would result in his lands becoming available, Lamb settled his debts and proposed to the Duchy that he should replace Gemmell as lessee. This proposal was recommended by Barrington, with Lamb promising to maintain the lands and building in good order. By the end of 1880, Lamb was in possession of all Gemmell's lands and, by 1882, was also leasing Prince Hall, where he settled.[67]

While Gemmell was still leasing Teignhead and before he left Devon for Middlesex, Peter Murray and his family were replaced at the farm by William Renwick, his wife Mary and son John.[68] A resident of Harford told of her father-in-law's memories of both Gemmell and Renwick:

"My father-in-law went to work when he left school at Woolwell Farm as a house boy, when he cleaned Mr Gemmell's shoes he use to give the thistle embossed on the toe of the shoe an extra polish. As he got older he was sent to Teignhead with a load of wooden sheep hurdles by horse and cart. When he got to go through a gate way the load was too wide to go through. He had to unload and load them again. When he arrived at Teignhead he was given a meal of boiled eggs boiled in the kettle then they made a pot of tea. My father use to tell me about the shepherds and their dogs, he mentioned a shepherd called Renwick who had a good dog called Clyde. They would bring the young sheep to Woolwell for the winter. Shepherds went back to Teignhead but dogs would stay with the sheep for a few days then go back to Teignhead on their own. The dogs were very clever. One would lead the flock others would stand at cross roads."[69]

By 1882, the Renwicks had moved out of the farm and James and Catherine Brown moved in. Their son, Robert, was baptised at Lydford Church in the March of that year. The parish registers show that by 1885, the Browns too had moved on and that Thomas and Mary Ferguson had become Lamb's tenants. While here, they had three children, William, Jane and Annie. It is probably the Fergusons to whom J.Ll.W. Page refers in his book *An Exploration of Dartmoor and its Antiquities*. The following quotation, gives a contemporary account of life at the farm:

"It is a wild place and the bare-headed children - and there are always a small tribe of them in and around a Dartmoor cottage - see so little of man that, after a prolonged stare at the stranger, they bolt into the house like scared rabbits. The Scotch shepherd, a communicative and intelligent man, will tell us of his troubles in the winter when the sheep get lost in the drifts, at the same time attacking with prodigious appetite, for he has just come back from Chagford, an immense chunk of the flesh of the aforesaid animal, while his stout and comely spouse lays a cloth upon the rough deal table and brings forth a large jug of milk - scalded; you seldom get raw milk upon Dartmoor - and cuts up enough of the staff of life for an Arctic expedition. Meanwhile the 'bairns', except the youngest who clings to mother's skirts, sit in a row upon a form by the great open chimney, and gaze with shy curiosity on the wayfarers, wriggling at the command to 'Take your fingers out of your mouth and speak to the gentleman'. A dog snores in front of the embers, and chicken congregate as near our chairs as they dare, hoping for, and generally obtaining, stray crumbs. An indescribable odour of peat-smoke and cream greets the nostrils, a curious but not unpleasant combination, because the door stands wide open, and the fresh Moor air which is driving the clouds so merrily across Sittaford Tor keep all things pure and fresh."[70]

A letter written by Lamb to the Duchy in 1884 further indicates that Manga Farm was by now in ruins. He states that a long dilapidated farmhouse in the Teignhead enclosures had lost its roof in a severe storm recently, and asks if he could use the materials from it to repair an outbuilding.[71] This has to be Manga Farm as it was the only other farm existing here.

As Lamb continued to breed sheep on Dartmoor, his initial difficulties with them must have been overcome. No difficulties whatsoever occurred when he permitted a small group of sheep to appear on stage in a pantomime held at the Plymouth Theatre Royal. Crossing comments that they "have proved themselves equal to the strain of a six week run, and won a round of applause each night. ... During the run of the pantomime, the employees of Mr Lamb visited the theatre and were delighted at the admirable manner in which the curly coated little Dartmoor actors acquitted themselves."[72]

During 1889, James and Joanna Little, both from Scotland, replaced the Ferguson family at Teignhead. In 1983, John (Jack) Hamlyn, who was born in 1883, was interviewed by Dr Tom Greeves who made the following notes: "I asked Jack who was at Teignhead Farm when he first knew it and he said it was a Mr Little, a shepherd for Mr Lamb of Prince Hall. Jack went there first when he was six years old - he and his grandmother went to live there for a fortnight while Mr Little went away to Scotland for a holiday. A man came to milk the cows while they were there."[73]

On 3rd April 1893, James Lamb died. He left his wife Jane his estates on Dartmoor and she continued to manage them with the help of her son-in-law, Mr Colville.[74] In 1897, Little left Teignhead and Mrs Lamb sub-let the farm to Mr James Brock. For about a year, Mr James Clark also lived at the farm with Brock.[75] Brock's bachelor status caused Mrs Lamb some concern. She felt he needed a wife to look after him and took it upon herself to advertise for one! Having

Teignhead Farm photographed by Robert Burnard on 12th August 1889.

chosen a likely applicant, Mrs Lamb met her at a local station and conducted an interview. Deeming the girl a suitable candidate for the vacancy of wife, Mrs Lamb gave her the position! She must have met with Mr Brock's approval because he married her.[76] This story was related to the author by a Chagford man, and it is also alluded to by H.G. Michelmore when he wrote that the shepherd at Teignhead Farm "had married his wife through a matrimonial advertisement. When his life partner arrived, the Shepherd found she was a large rawboned Scotswoman of physical strength beyond his own."[77]

Mrs Brock, was a stout woman by all accounts. She gave birth to several babies, and of those delivered by the midwife, none survived. The two Mrs Brock delivered herself - both boys - lived. Due to the remoteness of the farm, the children, George and Reg, would run and hide if visitors came, in much the same way as the Ferguson children had in the 1880s. George met with an untimely death in an accident with a horse and cart in the 1920s and Reg died in the 1972 'flu outbreak. He had a cottage on Taw Green.[78]

Mrs Lamb gave up the lease on Teignhead Farm in 1900 and it was bought by William and Frank Hamblyn. Frank initially lived at Drewsteignton then moved in turn to Spreyton, Dunstone near Widecombe, Newton Abbot and then finally left Devon c.1916.[79]

Under Brock's occupation, sheep farming declined and cattle once more became the main type of livestock reared. His buying and selling was undertaken by Mr Perryman of Chagford and in 1904, Galloway heifers were brought to the farm.[80]

It was during Brock's tenancy that the practice of serving teas to the public became established, a tradition that was to continue with other tenants. James Perrott had installed a post box out at Cranmere Pool in 1854, and during the latter part of the nineteenth century, visits to Cranmere from Chagford became popular. Perrott died in 1895, but his sons, John and Stan continued to take visitors out there in horse-drawn carriages via the Fernworthy road to Teignhead Farm from where the visitors would walk the rest of the way. On their return to the farm, teas would be served by Mrs Brock. This would have been a welcome addition to the farm's income. In the author's possession is an old postcard of the farm on which the correspondent tells of his trip to the "cottage" with Perrott as his guide.

The Perrotts were not the only people to organise trips out to Cranmere Pool as private parties of friends or relatives would also make their way out to Teignhead either by carriage or on foot from Chagford.

Fishing rights were rented out to people for the Teignhead stretch of the North Teign, and Mr Gilbert Spiller enjoyed many a day's fishing here during the Brocks occupation of the farm. He would visit the farmhouse for lunch. "One day he detected a very pleasant fragrance as he approached the cottage, and was regaled by the Shepherd's wife with a sumptuous meal of roast hare. This he much enjoyed, and on leaving he asked the woman in jest whether her old man had poached the hare, to which she replied, 'Oh, the master didn't catch he; I found 'un dead in the stream yesterday.'"[81]

Mrs Brock was not as houseproud as other women might have been. One of the kitchen drawers was home to a ferret,[82] and Hemery tells of how a pig is supposed to have lain under the kitchen table while refreshments were served to guests. Mr Brock it seems, enjoyed an occasional drink and used to ride his horse out to Princetown and frequent one of the public houses, succumbing somewhat to the influences of alcohol. It would appear that his wife was not prepared to turn a blind eye to his drinking sprees and "whenever he returned home showing any signs of dissipation, she used to flog him."[83]

Frank Hodge, who remembered Brock, said of him,

"He used to come in Princetown ... and he was as drunk as a fool. Little fellow he was. And he'd stay there until the policeman used to order him home. They didn't used to lock 'em up like they do now ... He'd stay there till he got ... he couldn't stand. And we boys used to get 'un out. Old policeman used to watch it - his boys was in it - he'd sot up be Plume of Feathers watching. We'd get 'un out from the Railway Hotel ... and pushed 'un in the cart with his backside out over like. And my cousin Bill Moses used to catch hold with his teeth his backside till he kicked and hollered like the devil. Used to roll 'un in

Mr and Mrs James Brock standing outside Teignhead Farm with Reg Collins (right). Two of the horses were named Actress and Tommy. c.1909.

the cart, put up the tailboard, and that horse would go, go right home to Teignhead, and he'd sleep all the way home. What about that then? ... poor old Jimmy."[84]

That Mr Brock had a fondness for alcohol is further illustrated by another tale told by H.G. Michelmore, and although he does not mention Brock by name, it can be assumed it is him as he is referring to the shepherd of the 'matrimonial advertisement'. Apparently, the Squire of Gidleigh, who happened to be the Chairman of the Moretonhampstead Bench too, would travel to the Petty Sessions on horseback. One day, while attending the Petty Sessions, he received an urgent message requesting him to visit a relative in Torquay. Meeting the Teignhead shepherd in Moretonhampstead, he asked him to take his horse back to Gidleigh for him.

"Unfortunately he accompanied the instruction with the gift of a shilling, and when the Shepherd had converted the sum into alcohol, he decided that it was a long walk from Gidleigh to Teignhead, so he rode the horse back to his own home. This conduct attracted a very severe hiding from his spouse, but when he had sobered down the next day he was afraid to ride the horse back to Gidleigh, and in due course the Squire had the pleasure of fetching the animal from the depths of the moor. Rumour had it that the Shepherd thereafter was very careful not to make any enforced appearance before the Moreton-hampstead Bench."[85]

As well as alcohol, it has been claimed Mr Brock also had a liking for raspberries and that he grew them in a hollow below Watern Coombe, calling the place 'Raspberry Garden'. Although not impossible, this does sound rather unlikely, especially when there was a vegetable garden just opposite the farmhouse!

The Brocks stayed at Teignhead Farm until 1914, leaving behind a large pile of ashes in the front room.[86] The new tenant was Mr John Hutchings from Belstone who farmed here until 1923 before which, in 1916, Mr Richard Amery of Withecombe in Chagford took over the lease from the Hamblyn brothers.

It has been claimed that Richard Amery's brother was joint lessee of Teignhead Farm,[87] but I found no evidence to support this. Thomas Amery farmed Beechlands at Chagford, but it is possible that he grazed his cattle at Teignhead during the summer months. In 1918 Richard Amery gave up the lease and it was acquired by Mr Ralegh Buller Phillpotts.[88] Tenant John Hutchings remained at the farm during the summer months and spent the winters at Laughter

Hall House. He also did part time work at Fernworthy and Bellever.

Mr Ralegh Phillpotts (later to become Sir Ralegh Phillpotts) was born in London in 1871, was educated at Winchester and Balliol College, Oxford and in 1898, married Miss Jean Stewart. In World War One, he served in the 1st Devon Yeomanry 1914 - 1916 and was Staff Captain in Eygpt in 1916. His favourite pursuits were hunting, shooting and riding,[89] so Dartmoor offered an ideal location for practising these. He took a lease on Laughter Hall House c.1915, which was built in 1912 by Mr Halfyard from Princetown. His permanent residence was at Rora House, Liverton near Newton Abbot. His daughter-in-law, Mrs Diana Phillpotts, said how much he loved the moor, and would often go out to Teignhead and spend a night or two at the farm. His son Alan, Mrs Diana Phillpott's husband, would also go out there in his school holidays.

The Final Era 1923 - 1980s

It is in 1923 that Teignhead Farm entered its final era. It was to be occupied by another Hutchings family who were descended from the original William Hutchings who lived here in the early 1800s. Members of this family were the last official occupants of this lonely farmstead. Sidney and Laura Hutchings moved into Teignhead Farm as Sir Ralegh Phillpott's tenants in 1923.[90] Sidney was born at Brimstonedown, Gidleigh in 1859, the son of William and Ann Hutchings. Born into a farming family, he too followed suit and, in 1881, was living and working as a herdsman at Livaton Farm near South Tawton, for John Tucker. He married Laura (known as Millie) and, while living at Belstone, their eldest son, George, was born. It was George who was to be the last tenant at Teignhead Farm. Other children followed; William Ernest, Maud and Millie. During the early 1900s, the Hutchings moved from northern Dartmoor down south to Higher Brimley Farm near Bovey Tracey, and here they stayed until their move to Teignhead.[91]

In addition to Sidney Hutchings as tenant, Sir Ralegh also employed Walter Hutchings as his Bailiff, and he spent the summers out at Teignhead where he tended the sheep, and returned to Ilsington in the winters where he had Pool Farm and the Willis Fields near Rora Woods.[92] It is he who appears in the Kelly's Directories and it is not unlikely that this was in fact the John Hutchings who had been living out at Teignhead since 1914. Apparently, 'John' was an alternative name for one of the Hutchings men. Also living at Pool Farm were John and Amelia Hutchings. Mrs Diana Phillpotts remembers Amelia as a very old lady; she was known as "Granny Hutchings" and lived in a "shack" at Pool, dying in 1949 at the age of 82. She had been a widow for 19 years. It is highly probable Walter was her son and that there is a family link between these Hutchings and those of Teignhead.

Sidney made his living at Teignhead by looking after other people's livestock - mostly cattle - and was paid a few pence per head. He claimed he made more money at Teignhead than he had ever made in his life![93] His income was further supplemented by continuing the practice of supplying cream teas to walkers, and there are still people today who remember this. Mrs Saunders, who was born in Chagford at the end of last century, and later moved to Drewsteignton, recalls her family outings to the farm, en route from Chagford to Cranmere Pool. At Teignhead they would change into plimsoll type shoes as they found these easier to walk in. The mires also made their shoes smell and plimsolls were easier to clean. Around the hems of their skirts, the ladies

Teignhead Farm mid 1930s.

would pin wide bands of protective material to guard against the mud.

Sidney had a long beard and reminded people of Moses, and was often found reading the family bible. He also enjoyed imbibing at the Chagford hostelries, sometimes returning home in quite a 'merry' state! Once, while returning after a night's cider drinking, he fell into a stream, was unable to get out, and spent the night there. On being helped home the following morning, he was put to bed and the doctor was sent for. Sidney was none the worse for his adventure and the doctor ordered brandy to be administered. However, his wife drank it instead![94] Laura is remembered as a large lady who wore a large bonnet and had a "dry temperament". Mrs Saunders recalls being told very sharply, "Don't do that missy!" for nothing in particular. She considered that every country girl should know how to pluck a goose, and therefore gave the young Mrs Saunders a lesson on how to do just that. She was also given two geese of her own to fatten up for the Michaelmas and Christmas dinner tables.

Memories of the interior of Teignhead are mainly of the kitchen. The ceiling was low with wooden beams on which the men had to be careful not to bang their heads. The floor was of stone upon which stood the large kitchen table with benches under, set up against the wooden partition, behind which was presumably

Teignhead Farm 1955.

still the dairy. There was also a settle. In the southern wall was the fireplace and hearth, and to the side was a sizable cupboard recess in which wood and faggots were kept. This recess with stonework shaped in a curve can still be seen amongst the ruins. A blacksmith in Chagford made the Hutchings a special iron baking oven to fit into the fireplace and Laura is remembered cooking on it. The general feel of the place was described to the author as "antique", and living conditions would have changed very little from the early days. The front door was very heavy wood and had studs on it. The thatched roof was replaced with slates in 1912,[95] and it was re-slated in the 1920s by Mr Stone of Chagford. The tall chimneys seen in the 1930s photograph were built to this height due to the frequent winds experienced out here. They helped ensure that the rooms remained smoke free from the open fires that were continually burning.

Outside in the courtyard was the dung pit. This was edged with smallish granite stones, and although overgrown today, is easy to locate. Over the dung went ashes from the fireplaces and, as Mrs Saunders commented, the area often smelt rather strong! She remembers the privy as being inside the little corrugated iron hut seen in the 1955 photograph taken by A.H.D. Davies. Opposite the front of the house is the walled garden area. This was tilled and used for growing fruit and vegetables such as peas and beans. There were also two apple trees. The Hutchingses kept a couple of pigs, a milking cow and poultry which would often be found in the courtyard.

Apart from the stone-built cattle sheds and outhouses near the house, Sidney Hutchings had erected a galvanised iron barn next to the linhay on the south wall of the house. Jim Endacott, who lived at Teigncombe and at Frenchbeer, remembered fetching the iron from Moretonhampstead railway station by horse and waggon. The whole exercise took a week.[96] The barn is likely to be the one to the left in the 1930s photograph. The small iron hut which stands in the courtyard today is made from some of this iron. Jim Endacott also recalled seeing the trees planted at Teignhead. These were felled in 1992 and approximately 54 rings could be counted on a cross section of one of the trunks, suggesting they were planted sometime around 1938.

It appears that Laura Hutchings did not bake her own bread, certainly not towards the end of her life at Teignhead. Instead, it was collected from Teigncombe Farm, usually by George. It was brought here by Mr Bill Daymond from the shop, 'Rowe's' in Chagford. There were also general shopping trips into Chagford by horse and cart,[97] although some of it was delivered out to Fernworthy from where it was collected.

Due to the farm's isolation, postal deliveries were not on a daily basis but two or three times a week. In the 1920s and early 1930s, they were on Tuesdays and Fridays. Then this changed but local memory conflicts as to the exact days - some say Mondays, Wednesdays and Fridays while others say Fridays only. A van would be driven out to Fernworthy and from there the postman would go on horseback to Teignhead Farm. He once became badly 'misted' on his return journey but fortunately, the horse knew his way back again. During the 1930s, when Fernworthy Reservoir was being built, the road to Fernworthy was diverted north of the original one and, once Fernworthy Farm was abandoned, a route via Batworthy would have been used.

In the early 1920s, one of Sidney's daughters gave birth to a baby girl, E. M. Hutchings. An elderly resident of Chagford remembers the child running and hiding behind the kitchen settle when visitors arrived, as she was not used to seeing many people.

She was unknowingly carrying on the 'tradition' practised by the Ferguson and Brock children.

The girl of course, had to be educated, but she was 8 before she was sent to attend school in Chagford. The entry in the school Log Book for 7th October 1931 reads "Admitted E. Hutchings aged 8 from Teign Head Farm. She has never attended any school - the distance being about 7 miles. She is boarding with a family in Chagford - the cost being partially met by a grant of £10 a year from the D.C.G.C."[98]

The following January, the Log Book records "E. Hutchings from Teign Head has 'mumps', therefore she'll not be able to come into school this month."[99] Sidney's name was given as her legal guardian, and she left school in 1937 and went into domestic service.

In 1933, Sidney and Laura Hutchings moved from Teignhead Farm to O'er Hill Cottage in New Street, Chagford,[100] leaving George at the farm, now in the employ of Sir Ralegh Phillpotts and therefore responsible for the running of the place. The Hutchings daughter Millie moved with them, and Maud shortly afterwards married Albert Aplin and went to live at Rose Cottage in New Street. They later moved to Holly Meadow and then Orchard Meadow. William Ernest worked as a gardener in the Totnes area and never lived at Teignhead. Both Sidney and Laura lived to a good age. Sidney died on 4th December 1952, aged 93, while Laura died on 28th August 1955, aged 94.

Finding himself alone now, with the exception of the summer months, George employed a housekeeper, Olive Dempster to look after him.[101] She stayed at Teignhead Farm until 1938. George is remembered as being a morose and taciturn character. He had served in the Devonshire Regiment during World War One and was on active service in Mesopotamia,[102] before returning to England and Higher Brimley Farm.

There are several recollections of George while he lived out at Teignhead. One is of a storm about to break while a father and son were on Whitehorse Hill. They made haste to the farm where they asked George if they could shelter in his barn. He deliberated for a long time before eventually allowing them to take cover. On one occasion, the same people were near Batworthy one December evening at sunset, when they saw George returning from Chagford with his Christmas supplies. A large sprig of holly protruded from his purchases, and the scene became silhouetted against the glow of the setting sun as he rode home along the track.[103] John Hamlyn, mentioned above, remembers that the first wireless he ever heard was at Teignhead Farm when George was there.

In 1939, when World War Two broke out, extensive tracts of Dartmoor became used for the training of both American and British troops. The land on which Teignhead Farm and newtake were situated was required by the War Department and, on 12th November 1942, it was requisitioned by them.[104] George Hutchings had to vacate the farm by Lady Day 1943, and he went to live at Lumhay, Holy Street near Chagford. He removed his furniture by horse and cart to a barn at Fernworthy from where he collected them later.[105] Walter Hutchings no doubt farmed at Pool Farm the entire year round from then on.

The farmhouse underwent some damage during the military occupation. The army kept ammunition in the outhouse, and a resident of Chagford recalls bullet holes in the masonry caused by small arms fire. On 29th September 1950, the farm and newtake were de-requisitioned, and the then War Office had to pay compensation to the Duchy for the damage incurred.[106] From this date until 1984, the farm and newtake were leased to R.J. and J. Rowe of Frenchbeer Farm.[107] Neither lived in the farmhouse. Sir Ralegh

Phillpotts was approaching 80 so would not have wanted to renew his lease on the farm. In fact, he died in October 1950.

George Hutchings continued to live at Lumhay until his death in February 1960 at the age of 74. He was buried in Chagford churchyard.

As already established, George Hutchings was the last official resident and moorman to live at Teignhead Farm. Unofficially, the story of its occupation is not quite over. Photographs and recollections of the house in the 1950s and 1960s indicate it was in a fair state of repair externally. Hemery's photograph of it in his *High Dartmoor* is captioned 1952 and shows it with missing windows, door, masonry and porch roof tiles. A.H.D. Davies photograph of 1955, included in this chapter, shows the exterior more or less intact but with no evidence of recent repair, so it seems that Hemery's date must be erroneous.

The outhouse or cattle shed remained in good condition until the 1960s, and Mr Richard Waller remembers riding out to the farm with friends during the early 1960s and stabling their ponies in it. About this time, a young man, R.H., who loved the moor, took an interest in the farmhouse and decided it

Teignhead Farm 1968.

would make an ideal retreat. Technically R.H. was a squatter as he did not obtain permission from the Duchy to use the building. The floorboards were no longer safe upstairs so he made a downstairs room habitable and replaced a window and a door.[108] Chagford people remember R.H. riding out to Teignhead on his motorbike, taking planks of wood for repair jobs with him! He also took wood from Fernworthy Forest, and apparently had deliveries of peat made for his open fire.[109] The room he renovated had an arm chair and a television run on a battery.[110] R.H., it seems, rode out to Teignhead via Fernworthy Forest on Friday evenings and stayed there until Monday mornings, when he departed for work at Sam Harris' scrapyard in Chagford.[111] He kept cats,

and on the Monday mornings, he would leave a supply of food for them with the intention of it lasting until the Friday![112] While at Teignhead, R.H. would tend Jack Rowe's livestock grazing in the newtake.[113] When not working, he would stay at Teignhead during the week as well. It is possible that his diet was supplemented by rabbit meat as wild rabbits were a common sight here until about 1970, when their numbers declined.

That R.H. did not like " trespassers" is also recalled by local people. He erected notices saying "Private. Trespassing Forbidden" and "Keep Out". Could one of these be appearing face downwards in Hemery's photograph? Obviously, R.H. did not consider himself to be a trespasser on the Duchy's land.

The ruins of Manga Farm today.

The well-made hut built within the ruins of Manga Farm, 1988.

Towards the end of the 1960s, R.H. lost interest in the farmhouse. With no one to look after it, it quickly fell into disrepair and became a target for vandals. Mr Eddie Hain, a former National Park Ranger for the area, told how, in 1970, the roof slates fell off in one go. He tried to get the relevant authorities to retrieve the slates but they left it too late and they were stolen.

A tractor and trailer were probably brought out there to remove them. With the roof gone, the decay quickened, and demolition took place in early 1971, the Duchy bringing in contractors to knock it down.[114] Mr Tom Hutchings of Chagford says that the first contractor approached could not get his equipment out to the farm building. Hence another contractor did the deed, marking the end of this farmhouse's fascinating social history.

Manga Farm had, of course, been in ruins for decades. But the late 1980s saw it partially 'occupied' by a squatter - a young girl with two dogs. In February 1988, the well constructed, one-roomed hut within the walls of what was once Manga Farm's kitchen was clearly visible.[115] The girl is reputed to have stayed out there for two winters before moving on. When her hut was taken down, the contents were revealed and comprised a handmade wooden bedstead, stool, table and an item for cooking on over the little fireplace. All traces of her stay are now gone. The original fireplace is less discernible now and more granite rubble fills the interior.

REFERENCES
1. DCO (L). Lease Book 1807-11. 1st February 1808 and 13th May 1808
2. loc. cit.
3. loc. cit.
4. Crossing, W. *Crossing's Guide to Dartmoor* David & Charles 1976 (reprint of 1912 ed.) p.239 and Crossing, W. *The Teign from Moor to Sea* Quay Publications (Brixham) 1986 (printed in book form from *Western Morning News* 1900) p.6
5. Starkey, F.H. "A Misplaced Dartmoor Farm" in *Odds and Ends from Dartmoor* privately published 1984 p.65
6. Parish Registers, Gidleigh
7. DCO(L) Box 55. Teignhead Farm docket. Letter: 3.8.1852
8. For example, Hemery, E. *High Dartmoor* Robert Hale Ltd 1983 p.813 and Starkey, F.H. op. cit. p.65
9. DCO(L) "Plan of the Forest of Dartmoor. The Property of HRH the Prince of Wales describing the Several Newtakes". c.1802-4
10. DRO (Exeter) Ref. Z17/3/8. Simpson, W. "Survey of the Forest of Dartmoor belonging to HRH the Prince of Wales" 1786
11. DRO (Exeter) Ref. Mason Tucker papers 924B/B1/8
12. loc. cit.
13. loc. cit.
14. loc. cit.
15. Somers Cocks, J.V. "The Boundary of the Forest of Dartmoor on the North-Eastern Side" in *DCNQ* Vol 30 pp.284-7
16. "Bounds of the Forest of Dartmoor" in *TDA* Vol 24 p.422
17. Greeves, T. Letter to author: 1.12.1991
18. Hemery, E. op. cit. p.817
19. Parish Registers, Lydford
20. DCO(L) Prince Albert Council Minute Book 5th February 1842 - 30th March 1844 3.4.1843
21. DRO (Exeter) op. cit.
22. loc. cit.
23. loc. cit.
24. DCO(L) Box 55. Memorandum 1871
25. Worth, R.H. *Worth's Dartmoor* David & Charles reprint 1981 p.367
26. Vancouver, C. *General View of the Agriculture of the County of Devon* 1808 reprinted David & Charles 1969 p.120
27. British Museum, The, Letter to author: 22.1.1991
28. Baring-Gould, S. *Devonshire Characters and Strange Events* The Bodley Head Ltd 1926 p.175
29. DCO(L) Lease Book 1818-1825
30. loc. cit.
31. Somers Cocks, J.V. "Exploitation" in *Dartmoor: A New Study* David & Charles 1970 p.258
32. Tithe Apportionment, Lydford
33. DCO(L) Prince Albert Council Minute Book op. cit. 16.3.1843
34. DCO(L) Box 55. Letter: 22.6.1843
35. ibid. Report of Mr Shillibeer 25.10.1844
36. ibid. Letter: 24.3.1843
37. ibid. Letter: 20.3.1848
38. ibid. Letter: 5.12.1848
39. ibid. Letter: 26.9.1849
40. Baring-Gould, S. *A Book of Dartmoor* Methuen & Co 1900 p.164
41. DCO(L) Box 55. Letter: 26.9.1849

42. ibid. Letter: 29.7.1850
43. ibid. Letter: 26.8.1852
44. ibid. Letter: 2.9.1852
45. Inventory of Goods & Chattels of Teignhead Farm. Brought to author's attention by T. Greeves
46. Crossing, W. *The Teign from Moor to Sea* op. cit. p.6
47. DCO(L) Box 55. Letter: 21.4.1877
48. ibid. Letter: 8.2.1875
49. DCO (B) Letters Received Book: 6.4.1876
50. Hemery, E. op. cit. p.818
51. DCO(L) Box 55. Letter: 25.9.1876
52. ibid. Letter: 29.11.1876
53. loc. cit.
54. DCO(B) Teignhead Farm docket. Letter: 8.11.1876
55. Crossing, W. *Crossing's Dartmoor Worker* David & Charles 1966 p.24
56. DCO(B) op. cit. Letter: 11.12.1876
57. ibid. Letter: 9.5.1877
58. ibid. Letter: 12.5.1877
59. ibid. Letter: 22.5.1877
60. DCO(L) op. cit. Letter: 15.3.1877
61. DCO(L) Lamb's Tenancies docket. Letter: 21.4.1879
62. DCO(L) Box 55. Letter: 20.11.1879
63. ibid. Letter: 3.12.1879
64. ibid. Letter: 20.11.1879
65. DCO(L) Lamb's Tenancies. Letter: 8.7.1880
66. ibid. Letter: 17.7.1880
67. ibid. Letter: 25.3.1882
68. Parish Registers, Lydford
69. Matthews, Mrs A.A. Letter to author: January 1992
70. Page, John Ll.W. *An Exploration of Dartmoor and its Antiquities* Sedley & Co 1889 pp.198-9
71. DCO(B) Letters Received Book: 3.3.1884
72. Crossing, W. op. cit. p.24
73. Greeves, T. Letter to author: 1.12.1991
74. Last Will and Testament of James Lamb
75. Electoral Registers, Lydford
76. Perryman, M. Oral info. 1988
77. Michelmore, H.G. *Fishing Facts and Fancies* Wheaton & Co 1946 p.72
78. Perryman, M. op. cit.
79. Electoral Registers, Chagford
80. Perryman, M. op. cit.
81. Michelmore, H.G. op. cit. p.73
82. Perryman, M. op. cit.
83. Michelmore, H.G. op. cit. p.72
84. Greeves, T. Letter to author: 1.12.1991
85. Michelmore, H.G. op. cit. p.73
86. Perryman, M. op. cit.
87. Starkey, F.H. "A Misplaced Dartmoor Farm" in *DCNQ* Vol 34 1981 p.148
88. DCO(P) Teignhead Farm docket
89. *Who's Who in Devonshire 1934* Wilson & Phillips p.207
90. Electoral Registers, Ilsington and Chagford
91. loc. cit.
92. Phillpotts, Mrs D. Letter to author: 14.1.1991
93. Hutchings, T. Oral info. 4.10.90
94. Richards, Mrs D. Oral info. 26.1.1993
95. PRO IR58/66261
96. Hain, E. Oral info. 11.1.1991
97. Daymond, Mrs W. Oral info. 4.10.1990
98. DRO (Exeter) Chagford School Log Book 1924-36
99. oc. cit.
100. Electoral Registers, Chagford
101. loc. cit.
102. Somers Cocks, J.V. Oral info. 1989
103. loc. cit.
104. DCO(P) Letter to author from Colin Sturmer: 28.3.1991
105. Richards, Mrs D. op. cit.
106. loc. cit.
107. loc. cit.
108. Waller, R. Oral info. 1989
109. Hutchings, T. op. cit.
110. loc. cit.
101. Owen-Evans, T. Oral info. 10.1.1991
112. Le Messurier, B. Letter to author: 4.10.1990
113. loc cit
114. DCO(P) Letter to author from Colin Sturmer op. cit. 28.3.1991
115. The author is indebted to Mr Graham Amhof who brought this to her attention, accompanying her out there in February 1988.

2. FOX TOR FARM
The first ten years 1807 — 1817

The attempts made to improve and enclose the moor had not gone unnoticed by a Dawlish gentleman, Mr David Gray, "late his Majesty's Secretary of Legation and Charge D'affaires at the Court of Saxony".[1] Intent upon taming a tract of land, he successfully applied to the Duchy of Cornwall to enclose an area in the Swincombe valley and to establish a "farmhouse with offices" within this enclosure. The farmhouse was to be Fox Tor Farm, found at SX 629 705, and standing at a height of 1230 ft (375m) above sea level.

On 24th June 1807, Gray was granted a 99 year lease on his chosen plot of 582 acres, at a rent of £28.5s.6d. Of this land, about 16 acres was deemed unusable due to the extensive presence of rocks and old tin workings. According to this lease, the actual bounds of Gray's land were "North and North East and East upon Scurhill; South East and East upon County Comb and Fox Tor Hill; South West and West upon the Plymouth Dock Leat and North West upon Steanan Hill and Fox Torr Brook." 'County Comb' was the stream now called the Swincombe.

Gray's enthusiasm for following agricultural pursuits in this location was short-lived and, a year later, the land changed hands, he in the meantime having moved to Teignmouth. Mr Thomas Windeatt from Bridgetown near Totnes, applied to take over the lease from 24th June 1808, and the Indenture was signed in February 1809.

According to Burt, who wrote the Introduction and Notes to N.T. Carrington's *Dartmoor*, work on the actual farm building did not begin until 1812. It is well known that Windeatt's workmen were instrumental in the destruction of Childe's Tomb, a prehistoric cairn in the Sand Parks area, upon which stood a granite cross, and a furious Burt wrote that Windeatt was responsible because he appropriated "some of the stones for building and door steps".[2] Crossing, who was also dismayed by this act of vandalism, claimed that some of the stones were also

Childe's Tomb before it was dismantled by the builders of Fox Tor Farm. This picture was drawn and etched by P.H. Rogers and it was published in Carrington's Dartmoor.

used in the construction of a footbridge over a stream between Fox Tor and the farm, which is what we call the Swincombe today. He enlisted the help of Richard Eden, a one-time occupier of the farm, to locate some of the stones from Childe's Tomb, and also the tomb or cairn itself.

The search was successful; nine of the twelve pedestal stones were located, together with the broken socket stone. By 1881, a cross head was found nearby by workmen repairing the newtake walls, and although it could never be proved that this once belonged to Childe's Tomb, Crossing cherished the

The ford and collapsed clapper over the Swincombe near Fox Tor Farm.

fond hope that this, together with the other stones, would be incorporated into the eventual restoration of the cross. Indeed, this cross was repaired, with the help of Mr Fearnley Tanner and the Dartmoor Preservation Association, of which he was Hon. Secretary, but to Crossing's dismay, they set up "on a few of the stones thrown over the kistvaen, a new base and a new cross! ... it would have been far better had it been left untouched."[3]

Some of the newly found pedestal stones remained in service as a bridge over the Swincombe. The new base and cross were cut at Holne in 1885 and the broken, original socket stone can be found near the restored cross.

Of Windeatt himself, Crossing cannot be said to be complimentary, saying that his only achievement was to alienate the land from the commoners. Commenting further, he said, "whether the money which it used to be said he was in the habit of concealing in the crevices of Cumston Tor was the fruits of his work at Fox Tor Farm we are unable to say, but we should judge it to be extremely doubtful. Perhaps he was a prudent man, and became convinced after a short season of experimentalising that his cash, though yielding no return, would, at all events, be much safer in its rocky depository than invested in such an undertaking as the reclamation of Dartmoor."[4]

However, writing from his South Brent home to a local paper on this subject, and likening Windeatt's use of Cumston Tor to a bank, he said, "I think I am safe in saying that his investment paid quite as well as the majority of undertakings which have from time to time been carried on on the moor, and perhaps better as he doubtless saw his money back again."[5]

It is difficult to visualise how the completed farmhouse might have appeared, and there are conflicting ideas on the matter. According to Crossing, it was fairly impressive. "It was built for a gentleman's residence and Mrs Mortimer ... remembers the stables there, which were beautifully paved."[6]

However, Duchy records show that, certainly before 1857, the house had only a kitchen and a bedroom on the ground floor and space under the thatched roof. This space must have been used as extra sleeping accommodation, given the large numbers of occupants that sometimes inhabited the farm. As Barrington lived nearby, he was able to give the Duchy's London office first hand information on what was happening on their land. His contemporary accounts, rather than ones based on oral information given long after the event, are the most reliable.

Access to the farm was via a track that came over Ter Hill, following the line of the crosses, from the Holne and Hexworthy districts. Says Crossing, "I have learned in the neighbourhood that when the farmhouse near Fox Tor was built, the timber used in its construction was drawn to its site by a team of oxen along this route."[7]

No doubt the timber came from Brimpts, from where much of the timber used on the moor came. There was also access to the farm from Whiteworks and a track ran from this mining settlement across the River Strane, through a hunting gate in the Tor Royal wall to the ford on the Swincombe, the former being known as Stream Hill Ford. The track then went up the hill to the farmhouse. Slate for the roof is reputed to have been brought to the farm by this route.[8]

The Tithe Map indicates that most of the land surrounding the house was used for arable purposes. In addition, there was a meadow, a small potato plot to the south of the house and a "coarse piece". The remaining enclosed field was "moor". Outside these fields, the land was uncultivated moorland. The livestock kept at the farm were cattle. A potwater leat would have supplied the farm with a water. There is a ditched boundary immediately above the farm, running along the contour of the hill, and this looks as though it could have served as the channel for a leat, but its actual head weir is not clearly defined. If a leat, it could easily have brought potwater to the farm itself, but the field evidence is not conclusive.

On the hill slopes in the immediate vicinity of the farm, and in particular to the north, there are numerous rocks that have been shattered by blasting. The distinctive long drilled shot-holes are clearly visible. This unusual sight is likely to be linked with the proximity of Whiteworks Mine and a ready supply of gunpowder. Some of the blasted stone has been built into field boundaries associated with the farm.

The area at the north eastern boundary corner of the farm is known as Mount Misery and the cross which stands just inside the gateway is called Mount Misery Cross or Foxtor Newtake Cross. The area was apparently named Mount Misery by a Scottish farmer who grazed his sheep here, and who did not do too well. This may have been Scotsman Mr James Lamb, or one of his shepherds, who grazed Scottish Blackface sheep here in the 1880s.

The Edens 1817 - 1859

Windeatt did not stay many years at Fox Tor Farm, and by 1817, it was occupied by moorman Jeffrey Eden and his wife Mary.[9] It is not clear when Windeatt actually relinquished his lease on the farm, but ownership is attributed to him in a map accompanying the Tor Royal Estate Sale Catalogue of 1828. But by 1840 the lease had passed into the hands of Mr William Wingate, who had various other pockets of land in the area, and was joint lessee with Mr George Bouvay for one piece of land used by the Edens.[10]

While living at the farm, Jeffrey and Mary completed their large family of at least ten children, and it is to one of their sons, Richard (Dick), who also became a moorman, that Crossing often refers.

Throughout the records consulted, the spelling of the name Eden varied; for example, Aden, Eden, Hayden, Haydon etc. 'Eden' is the spelling commonly used, and it is used here.

Jeffrey Eden employed farm labourers on the farm, one of whom worked on a daily basis, returning home each evening. This was the father of Crossing's friend, Richard Cleave of Hexworthy. Writing in 1903, Crossing said that the "late Richard Cleave ... once told me that his father spaded many acres of land at Fox Tor, in the early part of the last century, and that he was paid 4d a yard for the work."[11] Spading was a method of taming the land by paring and burning, making it suitable for cultivation. Another labourer was Samuel Parr who lived with the Edens at Fox Tor Farm with his wife, Marianne. While there, in 1833, she gave birth to their first daughter, also named Marianne, and in 1835, to their first son, William.

This Samuel Parr was the squatter who, some time before 1840, set up home on the opposite side of the Swincombe in an old tinners' hut, having erected a roof over the top. (Inside, surrounded by an incised border, are carved the initials and date I C 1753). Today it is known as Sam Parr's House. The land on which the hut stood was also leased from the Duchy by Wingate,[12] so was Sam Parr really the squatter he is reputed to have been, or a tenant paying rent to Wingate for his shelter, as the Edens did for Fox Tor Farm?

Sam Parr's House.

From the 1841 census returns, it is clear that the Parrs were still here and had named their dwelling 'Stream Cottage'. Described as an agricultural labourer, he no doubt still worked for the Edens. By 1851, they had moved to Beardown Cottage and the 1881 census returns see them at Blackabrook where Sam was described as a farmer of 6 acres. By this time, he and Marianne had 8 children. One of Jeffrey Eden's labourers was his son-in-law John Hamlyn, who married his third daughter, Margaret in February 1841. He too lived at the farm and a daughter Elizabeth was born to them in the June of that year.

Accommodation at Fox Tor Farm in the 1830s must have been very cramped with so many Eden children and the lodgers and their offspring. This burden was increased when, in 1836, one of Jeffrey's daughters, Maria, gave birth to an illegitimate son, Richard. Then in 1838, another daughter, Elizabeth, gave birth to an illegitimate daughter, Sarah. No clue is provided in the parish registers as to whom Richard's father was, but little Sarah was given the name of Hannaford, a common Dartmoor surname. This child was not to remain long without a father because, in 1841, Elizabeth married that notable stone wall builder, John Bishop. Sadly, further searches through the records show that history repeated itself. Sarah, at the age of 20, gave birth to an illegitimate daughter, Fanny Malinder. Both appear in the 1861 census returns for the Tavistock Workhouse.

In 1840, there was a proposal to build a railway between Plymouth and Exeter via Chagford. Some of the track was to have been laid through the Swincombe valley, affecting a portion of Fox Tor Farm's land, together with the immediate vicinity of Sam Parr's House, described in the plans as "Dwelling House and Garden".[13] Picturesque as the locomotive journeys might have been, it could be considered fortunate by some that this scheme did not get off the ground.

The Eden household became smaller in the 1840s, some of the children leaving home together with the lodgers, but Richard was still there working as an agricultural labourer. On 6th October 1848, he married Nancy Tamlyn of Swincombe Farm/Lodge (which was originally built as a fishing retreat). Nancy had begun life at Merripit in Postbridge, the daughter of tin miner, John Tamblyn. It is likely that Richard's married life began at Swincombe as a Richard Hayden [ie. Eden] appears in the 1851 census

returns. His wife is recorded as Mary but mistakes of this nature were unfortunately common in the returns. The two children attributed to them co-incide with entries in the parish registers. Between 1849 and 1871, Nancy produced at least 12 children.

After Jeffrey Eden's death in the 1840s, his son William (who had been living with his wife, Sarah, in Buckfastleigh) and his widow, Mary, made an application to the Duchy to lease the farm at an annual rent of £10, indicating that Wingate had since given up the lease which was acquired by Jeffrey in 1843.[14] This application was granted to them in April 1847. The following May, the Edens were experiencing difficulties. Mr Edmunds and Mr Creber, the Forest Renters, were demanding payments of £5 and £2. 10s. respectively if their cattle strayed beyond the limits of Fox Tor Farm. Mrs Eden, unable to afford this, suggested that the rent might be reduced by £5 to allow her to pay. Luckily the Duchy instructed Edmunds and Creber not to demand rent or impound her cattle should they stray.[15]

The Dartmoor climate took its usual course with an isolated and exposed farmstead. In the summer of 1848, William and Mary Eden declared Fox Tor Farm as more or less uninhabitable and they informed the Duchy that they would be compelled to leave unless repairs were undertaken. If a lease of 7 years was granted to them, they would be willing to carry out the repairs themselves. Inspecting the farm, Barrington found that "it will be quite impossible for the tenants to occupy the House much longer, every part of the House is untenable."[16]

Consequently, the Edens terms were met and, in 1849, William further agreed to erect a new chimney and repair the thatched roof. In 1851 more repairs were needed, and were this time carried out by Mr Edward Caunter of Princetown for £45. 10s.

During William Eden's tenancy, carpenter John Millman and his wife, Mary Ann, lodged at the farm and in 1854 their son James was born here. It is likely Millman was a mine carpenter at Whiteworks.

Not long after William's lease had expired, the farm was again in a state of disrepair. In April 1857 Barrington described it as uninhabitable and, no doubt, the Edens agreed. It would appear that the Edens were not always willing to keep the thatched roof in a state of good repair. In *Worth's Dartmoor*, Worth states,

> "When a cottage at Fox Tor, a structure of no great age, was falling into grievous disrepair, it was occupied by Eden the moor-man, and its roof was patched in any way and all ways, including turves. A visitor to the moor took shelter there during a thunderstorm, and found the roof leaky, and the shelter but partial. He asked Eden why he did not patch the roof. Said Eden: 'Who's going thatching in this weather?' Eden was told he could thatch it when it was fine, but replied: 'Who's to waste fine weather filling holes that ain't hurting?'"[17]

Barrington proposed several alterations to the farm in 1857. He suggested that the kitchen and bedroom walls be raised by 3 feet (0.9m), and a slate roof erected to replace the thatch. This would give sufficient space for two bedrooms on the upper floor. The present bedroom on the ground floor could then be converted into a dairy.[18]

An estimate for these alterations was submitted by Edward Caunter, and it is from this we learn that the farmhouse measured 27 feet long and 16 feet wide (8.2m x 4.9m). Caunter suggested that as well as a new staircase, there should be new windows, doors and chimneys. This would cost £33. The Edens then asked to have "the house behind the dwelling covered",[19] which measured 33 feet long and 12 feet wide (10.1m x 3.7m) and was presumably the linhay. This, together with repairs to the kitchen floor and those already stated, would cost £45. 10s. No reference has been found to these repairs being done, but there was no further mention of the thatched roof in the records. Indeed, as previously mentioned, slate is reputed to have been brought to the farm via the Whiteworks track.

In the September of 1857 William's brother, Richard, took over the lease on Fox Tor Farm at a rent of £10 per annum. He expressed a desire to cultivate and improve the land and repair all the fences himself.

Summering stock in the neighbouring Whiteworks Mine area, had become something of a problem for local farmers, so Richard Eden broached the subject with Barrington who wrote the following to Mr Henry Bickford at Princetown. "Mr Richard Aden of Foxtor called upon me sometime since and stated that there were many very dangerous Pits within the limits of Whiteworks alias Wheal Industry Sett and that Farmers would not send their Stock to summer there unless the pits in question were secured."[20] The outcome of this matter could not be found in the records.

Richard and Nancy had, by 1859, produced several of their many children and one son, Richard, was, according to a census return, "Dumb and a lunatic" while another, John, was referred to as "a lunatic from birth". Richard died in 1874, aged nearly 17. The burden of a large dependant family together with the relentless Dartmoor climate and little income proved too much for Richard Eden. In the March of 1859, Barrington wrote to the Duchy informing them of Richard's intention to leave "on account of his family's being afflicted, he considers the situation unhealthy and that the rent is more than he can in future undertake to pay."[21] Enclosed with Barrington's letter was one from Richard Eden. Although the letter appears in Hemery's *High Dartmoor*,[22] it is fitting to include it here. It reads:

J.R. Gardiner Esq.   *Dartmoor*
                                                21st March, 1859
Dear Sir,
                        FOX TOR FARM
I beg to inform you that it is my intention to quit the farm at Michaelmas next 1859, on account of my family being so afflicted. I have a family of six children, three of them quite helpless they cannot help themselves to nothing or are likely they ever will be able to. One ten years old, one three years old and one two years old.
                I am Sir, Your obedient servant,
                        Richard Aden [signed]

The letter implies there was another child with a disability.

On vacating the farm, the Eden family moved to Hexworthy and, in 1863, Richard obtained permission from the Duchy to build a cottage, shippen and linhay on a piece of waste ground. In later years, they moved to Warmacombe near Buckfastleigh where Richard and Nancy died, Richard in 1894, aged 70 and Nancy in 1914, aged 83.

The Last Occupants 1859 - 1863

After the Edens departure from Fox Tor Farm, the house underwent more repairs, after which the Duchy advertised the farm for letting. Samuel Chaffe was granted the lease at an annual rent of £12. 5s. 6d. He did not live at the farm itself and he may have been the Samuel Chaffe who lived at Sweaton near Widecombe. Instead, he sub-let it to agricultural labourer, Richard Worth, and from the 1861 census returns, we learn that he lived here with his wife Selina and their two children, John and Harriet. Harriet was the last in a long line of children to be born at the farm. The couple's next child was born at Powder Mills.

It is possible that the Worth's baby, Harriet, is the one to whom Tom Greeves refers in his *Tin Mines and Miners of Dartmoor*. He records a story given to him by Mr W.F. Coaker, concerning a child that was born at Fox Tor Farm. Apparently, it was decided that if the husband, who was a tin miner at Whiteworks, should be at work when his wife went into labour, she would hang out a sheet between two bushes as a signal for him to come home if she needed his assistance. On the actual day, she did hang out a sheet as arranged, but it was so foggy that it could not be seen beyond a few yards. When the husband arrived home after work, he found that she had successfully delivered her own baby. This baby's surname is supposed to have been Worth. The baptismal records do not suggest that Richard Worth was a tin miner, but it could well be that he did part time work in some capacity at the mine. It was fairly usual for men to alternate between farm labour and tin mining.

The Worth's occupation of Fox Tor Farm was short-lived. By 1863 they had moved to Powder Mills where Richard worked as a waggoner,[23] and by 1870 they had moved to Whiteworks.

In 1863, the Duchy received an enquiry from Mr John Dunn about the farm as he wanted to lease the lands and to know whether there was an available building. But despite this enquiry, the Worth family was the last to be sheltered under the roof of Fox Tor Farm, and it subsequently fell into an irreparable state.

Ransom, Gemmell and Lamb
1874 - c.1900

Although the history of the occupation of the farmstead drew to a close in the 1860s, it is worth recording how the bad state of repair did not deter one man's desire to re-establish it as a thriving concern.

In August 1874 the Duchy received a letter from Mr Henry Ransom, who lived in London and wanted to take over Chaffe's lease on Fox Tor Farm.[24] He would undertake not only to mend all the fences, but to build a substantial dwelling house at a cost of not less than £500, and repair the old cottage and linhay. On the farmland he proposed to grow turnips, oats, greens and pasture, and also have a rabbit warren, leaving a

A gatepost at Fox Tor Farm showing the wedge marks made when the granite was spilt.

The ruins of Fox Tor Farm.

sufficient number of rabbits for the next lessee to continue this trade! He further suggested a term of a 60 year lease from Michaelmas 1874.

Despite a reminder from Ransom to the Duchy about his letter the following month, they had still not come to any decision about his application by the November of that year. This resulted in Ransom's withdrawal, saying he might renew his interest the following spring. But this interest was not renewed (maybe he had witnessed a Dartmoor winter) and in 1877, Chaffe, who was still leasing the land, was given

notice to quit, along with George Caunter who leased Joan Ford's Newtake.[25] The new lessee was John Gemmell, who also rented Teignhead Farm. Chaffe did not vacate the farm immediately, but stayed on until Lady Day 1878.

In 1879 Gemmell's rent for the farm had fallen into arrears and in December, the Ashburton auctioneers Sawdye, entered the farmland and took possession of 150 sheep.[26] Gemmell's continued arrears resulted in the bailiffs taking possession of his effects at Fox Tor Farm in February 1880, the rest of the sheep being removed on the 24th of that month, presumably to be sold. By the end of 1880, Mr James Lamb had been granted the lease of Fox Tor Farm and in 1881, undertook extensive repairs to the newtake walls. It was during these repairs that the cross head was found.

The term "newtake" seems to have been applied to the farm after the house was deserted, and may have been introduced when Lamb instructed the rebuilding of these walls. This was probably the job on which Edward Worth and John Hooper of Nuns Cross Farm were employed, and to which Hemery refers.[27] The eastern boundary wall is supposed to predate the farm, having previously formed one wall of a newtake belonging to Andrew and John Knight in the 18th century.

The lands of Fox Tor Farm are still leased out to local farmers, but the history of the farmhouse, which came to a close in the 1860s, shows that its occupation spanned a mere 50 years.

REFERENCES

1. DCO(L) Lease Book 1807 - 1811
2. Carrington, N.T. *Dartmoor: A Descriptive Poem* Hatchard & Son 1826 p169
3. Crossing, W. *The Ancient Stone Crosses of Dartmoor* J.G. Commin 1902 p94
4. West Country Studies Library (Exeter) Newspaper Cuttings
5. Crossing, W. "The Dartmoor Bank Ltd" *The Western Antiquary* Latimer & Son 1883 Vol 2 p135
6. Crossing, W. *Princetown - It's Rise and Progress* Quay Publications (Brixham) 1989 p37
7. Crossing, W. *The Ancient Stone Crosses of Dartmoor* J.G. Commin 1887 p67
8. Oral info. David German 1990
9. Parish Registers, Lydford
10. DRO (Exeter) Ref. DP 148
11. Crossing, W. *Crossing's Dartmoor Worker* David & Charles 1966 p29
12. DRO (Exeter) op. cit.
13. loc. cit.
14. DCO(L) Prince Albert Council Minute Book 5th Feb.-30th March
15. DCO(L) Box 48. Letter: 6.5.1847
16. loc. cit.
17. Worth, R.H. *Worth's Dartmoor* David & Charles 1967 p407
18. DCO(L) op. cit.
19. loc.cit.
20. DCO(P) Letters Sent 26th June 1857 - 28th July 1860. 8th March 1858. (info. T. Greeves 7.12.1992)
21. DCO(L) Box 48. Letter: 21.3.1859
22. Hemery, E. *High Dartmoor* Robert Hale Ltd 1983 p.356. Hemery claims this letter was written by a Michael Aden, but he misread the signature.
23. Parish Registers, Lydford
24. DCO(L) Box 48. Letter: 29.8.1874
25. ibid. Letter: 19.3.1877
26. DCO(L) Box 55. Teignhead Farm docket. Letter: 4.12.1879
27. Hemery, E. op. cit. p.338

3. JOHN BISHOP'S HOUSE

Although today known as John Bishop's House, Duchy of Cornwall records show that it was officially called Swincombe Ford Cottage, occupying the site nearest to the ford across the River Swincombe. The cottage can be found at SX 642 726, between Hexworthy and Princetown. It stands at a height of 1000 ft (305m) above sea level.

Tracing the origins of the cottage has proved difficult. The neighbouring Swincombe Farm formed part of Sir Thomas Tyrwhitt's Tor Royal Estate and had been built "to afford accommodation as a Fishing Retreat".[1] Swincombe Ford Cottage did not form part of this Estate and does not appear on lease or sale

John Bishop's House today. The blocked up window can be seen in the upper part of the end wall.

maps for the area well into the 1820s. A suggestion that the cottage may have been built on the site of a medieval longhouse must be questioned. There is no documentary or field evidence to support this, and no enclosure on the site exists on early maps, including the O.S. Surveyors Drawings 1802-3, which show neither house nor associated fields. There were three newtakes owned by the Knights in the 1700s - Swancombe, Swancombe Ford and Swancombe Head. But the abovementioned O.S. Drawings indicate that these were other enclosures existing in the area. It seems the two-storey thatched cottage was built c.1827 because the Duchy granted 21 year leases for the property, and it came up for renewal in 1848.

In 1831 parish registers show that Elizabeth Sparkes, wife of Henry, died here at the age of 60. So it is likely that it was Henry Sparkes who obtained the initial lease from the Duchy to build this now well-known landmark.

Henry Sparkes married Elizabeth Stancombe on 5th November 1797. They had four children, John, Mary, Charles and Sarah, all born between 1798 and 1805. After Elizabeth's death, Henry continued to live in Swincombe Ford Cottage and he is listed as occupier in the 1839 Tithe Map schedule. From this we learn that, apart from the house and garden, there were two arable plots and two pasture plots. It has been claimed that water was supplied by a potwater leat taken off the Swincombe, but it would have to have been dug a very long way up the Swincombe to

The outhouses and rear of John Bishop's House today.

stones. The track was the Tavistock to Ashburton (T/A) packhorse track, a trading route dating back to the Middle Ages. The track continues up the other side to Swincombe Farm, but before reaching this, there is a branch off to the right through the Swincombe Ford Cottage enclosures to the cottage itself. Coming from Princetown, the old Tavistock to Ashburton track would have been taken, going past Tor Royal and Bull Park, and out onto Royal Hill over what is now called "Conchies Road", having been partially upgraded by Conscientious Objectors during World War One. The track enters the Swincombe Farm enclosures where a T/A track guide stone is acting as one of the gateposts. It then passes through a stroll which leads to two imposing granite pillars which formed the eastern boundary of the Tor Royal Estate. Only one of these now remains in good condition. The track continues down to the River Swincombe and on the way is the turning left to Swincombe Ford Cottage.

There is another track that leads from between the Swincombe Farm and Swincombe Ford Cottage enclosure walls over to Prince Hall. A T/A track guide stone is doing service as a gatepost where this track opens onto Sherberton Newtake.

In 1841 Henry Sparkes is listed in the census returns as a tin miner and therefore may have worked nearby at Gobbett Mine. His eldest daughter, Mary was still living in the cottage with him. Two years later, Henry died at the age of 72.

Between 1843 and 1848, occupation of Swincombe Ford Cottage is not easy to determine with any certainty, as no firm documentary evidence has come to light. There would have been five years left on the lease granted to Henry Sparkes, and it could be that John Bishop moved into the cottage towards the end of 1843. He obtained a 21 year lease from the Duchy

contour round to the cottage, so it is more probable it was taken off the little unnamed stream, up river from the cottage, flowing into the Swincombe. There are leats in evidence here, although equally the tin workings in the vicinity would have needed leats too. A stream flows past the garden's south-western wall which could have been used for a water supply.

The garden path leading to the house was cobbled and these cobbles can still be seen underneath the vegetation. The house itself would have been a two-up, two-down dwelling with the kitchen on the lefthand side where the fireplace was situated against the outer wall. The upper bedroom also had a fireplace.

Access to the cottage was via either Hexworthy or Princetown. From Hexworthy an old track passes over the northern part of Down Ridge, called Gobbett Plain, to the Swincombe. Up until 1892, when a timber footbridge was constructed, the only way across this river was by the ford or the stepping in 1848 and from this date, the property could legitimately be called John Bishop's House.

John's father, Thomas Bishop, was born in Whitchurch and on 13th April 1814, he married a Buckfastleigh girl, Mary Pethybridge. Their son, Thomas, was born in the September. Moving to the parish of Holne, their daughter Mary was born five years later. It was in 1821 that John was born, at Michelcombe.

By 1837 Thomas and his family had moved to Little Sherberton Farm[2] and in May 1841 his son John married Elizabeth Eden, daughter of Jeffrey Eden of Fox Tor Farm, and they went to live at Dartmeet. John found employment as a farm hand and stone wall builder on the Brimpts and Huccaby estates and worked for these until the 1860s.[3] Elizabeth Eden had, in 1838, given birth to an illegitimate daughter, Sarah Hannaford, who therefore became John Bishop's step-daughter. She did not adopt his surname but kept that of Eden. Sarah did not live with John and Elizabeth initially, but lived with her grandparents and their family at Fox Tor Farm. The census returns of 1841 record her as Jeffrey's daughter, although by the 1851 returns, Sarah is living with John and Elizabeth and their daughter, Eden Ann.

The relationship between John Bishop and his step-daughter is unknown but it was possibly strained. At some stage, as did her mother, Sarah became pregnant outside wedlock and left the area. Her daughter, Fanny Malinder, was born c.1860 in Exeter and six months later, they appear in the 1861 census returns for the Tavistock Union Workhouse where Sarah's occupation is given as domestic servant. It seems she may not have had moral and financial support from John and Elizabeth, and she disappears from records suggesting she died young or moved away. It was perhaps the former as Fanny went to live with John and Elizabeth, appearing in the 1871 and 1881 census returns.

It was in 1843 that John's own daughter, Eden Ann, was born. The parish records show that he and Elizabeth had moved from Dartmeet to Little Sherberton with Thomas and Mary, from where they moved across to Swincombe.

Although described as an agricultural labourer in the records, John Bishop is best known for his skills as a stone wall builder. In his *Dartmoor Worker*, Crossing devoted a chapter to the newtake wall builder and says that the walls are "formed of stones piled to a height of about four or five feet, and in some cases more, no mortar, not even turf being used."[4] All the builder needed to do was to collect the stones required, "and upon the size of these, of course, depended the character of his wall". Crossing also maintained it was John Bishop who was one of the first to introduce a new method of wall building whereby large stones were roughly squared and used in place of smaller ones. One such wall built by John Bishop is that of Muddilakes, running parallel with the B3357 road to Two Bridges. The tool he favoured for his stone walling was a crow bar or "bar ire"; "'tis surprisin' what you can do with a laiver or two". Transportation of suitable stones to the site of a wall was in the form of a sledge. "He was fond of praising the performances of a certain pony with one of these carriages. 'He belonged to my vayther', he used to say, 'an' wudden no more'n vourteen, or vourteen an' a half, an' I've a zeed'n shift a stone up dree tin wight 'pon a sledge'. When asked if he really meant to say that a pony of such size could draw so heavy a weight, he would answer, 'Ees; 'pon a sledge I tell you'".[5]

That John Bishop was good at his work cannot be doubted. Says Hamlyn Parsons, "By modern standards, old John was a reactionary stick-in-the-mud, but he was a craftsman and did many a good walling and draining job on the moor - and woe betide the employer who tried to teach him his job! He'd not get John again. He disliked new-fangled notions, and carried this to the extent of continuing to use flint and steel long after matches were on the market at a reasonable price ... but he could pass any job of his without blushing. He was the aristocracy of craftsmanship."[6]

There has been a suggestion that it was John Bishop who was responsible for building the porch on his cottage, but no relevant records have come to light to substantiate this; only a mention in relatively recent books for which no source is given. Perhaps the original author said this as a result of speculation, which may be quite justified.

John Bishop also farmed his own land of course, but this was on a small scale with probably just a few head of cattle, a domestic pig or two and some poultry.

Drainage work was also one of John Bishop's jobs for which he had a good reputation. However, his attempts to partially alleviate the extensive mires of Aune Head to secure better grazing for cattle were rather unfruitful. Crossing reminisced that "Cattle have frequently been lost in the mire at Aune Head, and I remember seeing old John Bishop of Swincombe in the summer of 1879 [he was only 53!] cutting a trench in it, for the purpose of draining it somewhat. ... This did not seem to be very effective."[7]

Another string to John Bishop's bow may have been poaching, although to be fair, the case against him was never proved. In December 1859, Charles Barrington accused him, along with Edward Caunter and William Pawley, of poaching hares on the moor. John was consequently told to "determine his tenancy" and, highly indignant of the accusation, complained to the Duchy, the result of which was to have his accusation withdrawn, with no further action taken.[8]

In 1866, John Bishop applied to the Duchy for him and George Caunter to increase the holding of his cottage by enclosing land on Swincombe Plain. Three years later when his lease came up for renewal, John requested an additional piece of adjoining wasteland plus 6 acres belonging to the Sherberton Estate. The tenant at Sherberton, John Coaker, was agreeable to this on condition that his rent was reduced by £1. 10s. per year. The 6 acres in question were coarse grass, but John wanted to cultivate the land, and the Duchy were agreeable to this.

John's daughter, Eden Ann, married labourer Isaac Worth on 1st May 1872, and went to live with him at Peat Cot. In January 1873, their son James was baptised at Princetown Church; sadly Eden Ann died later that month. This family tragedy was compounded by the death of baby James two months later. Thus John Bishop lost his only natural child and grandchild. His step-granddaughter Fanny remained at his cottage with him and Elizabeth for several years until she married.

Details of John Bishop's life at Swincombe Ford Cottage, and his workmanship on the moor can only be gleaned in small detail, and includes Crossing's recollections in which he seems to have had a great respect for the man. That he applied himself well in order to make a living from the land can be ascertained by Barrington's recommendation to the Duchy that the lease be renewed in 1890, for he said that John Bishop had worked hard to make his land good.

Two years after the lease on the cottage had been renewed, his life came to an end on 19th February, 1892, at the age of 70. He was buried at Buckfastleigh.

It was also in 1892, after John's death, that a footbridge was erected across the Swincombe following a heavy flood, and the timber for this came from Sherberton Plantation. It was built largely for the benefit of the miners of Mary Tavy who walked from their village to the mines of Hooten Wheals and Hensroost, where they stayed for a working week before walking back to Mary Tavy.[9] This footbridge "in part realised the wishes of old John Bishop, who lived close by, and who seemed to think that when it was possible to drive over the Swincombe at this point, instead of through it, there would be nothing else wanted on Dartmoor."[10] What a pity he did not live to see it.

The lease on John Bishop's House was inherited by his wife Elizabeth, who remained here until the late 1890s when she went to live with her granddaughter Fanny who had married John Michael Pitton in the 1880s. She died here in 1903, aged 87 and was buried, not at Buckfastleigh with John, but at Princetown. The lease on John Bishop's House then passed to Fanny.

In 1896, there was a fire at John Bishop's House in which the thatched roof was lost and much damage done to the interior.[11] It is likely it was at this point that Elizabeth moved to Whiteworks. It has been claimed that the inhabitants escaped down an outside staircase, but this seems very unlikely. There is a granite buttress on the corner of the front of the cottage constructed of long stones but it does not lead down from any upstairs window. Elizabeth Bishop would have been 80 at the time and even to jump onto this buttress from an upstairs window would be highly improbable. The cottage was rebuilt and a slate roof replaced the burnt thatch. There is a blocked up window on an upper side wall, and this may have been done at the time of the repairs. An outside privy was also erected c.1899.

When Elizabeth moved to Whiteworks, John Bishop's House was sub-let to William Coaker[12] whose Coaker relatives had the farms of Swincombe and Sherberton. William lived here with his family until 1908 when he moved to Nuns Cross Farm,[13] built in 1901 by Edward Worth. While living at John Bishop's House, William's wife gave birth to Elizabeth Ann in 1899 and to William Frank in 1906.[14] He was the last baby to be born here. Elizabeth married Percy Ware of Ditsworthy Warren where they lived before building their bungalow near Burracombe Ford. This was, in later years, used as a Scout Hut and then pulled down in the late 1980s to be replaced with a two storey adventure training centre.

Hemery cites Elizabeth Coaker's childhood memory of her mother chasing off a pack of hounds who were worrying a ewe on the bridge over the Swincombe. She did this "single-handed and armed with a hastily grabbed stick."[15]

When the Coakers moved to Nuns Cross Farm, William retained an interest in John Bishop's House and let Henry Worth live in it.[16] By 1911, Worth was living at Peat Cot but still rented it from Coaker. It was in this year that Fanny's lease on the property expired and it was bought from the Duchy by Thomas Coaker.[17] No further reference to the house being lived in again has been found and, in fact, c.1911, a document reveals that "The dwelling house has recently been turned into shippens"[18] showing that it had changed from domestic to agricultural use for Thomas working on the next door farm.

In 1912, a new Swincombe Farm was built next to the old one and into this moved James and Elizabeth Chudley who had been living at Gobbett Cottage.[19] Thomas Coaker left the old Swincombe Farm in 1914.[20] It could be that when the outbuilding for the new Swincombe Farm was built a couple of years after the

John Bishop's House, c.1950s.

John Bishop's House, 1968.

new house, the stone from the old farm was used. Substantial remains of the outbuilding are still standing. A John Chudley is recorded as living at Swincombe for the years 1918 and 1919.[21] He probably lived with James and Elizabeth.

And so the social history of John Bishop's House comes to a close during these early years of the twentieth century. The cottage became dilapidated and the decaying process accelerated during the 1970s when the roof fell in, the first floor joists collapsed and the back wall of the cottage and the attached outbuildings gave way. Today it is a rubble-filled shell, but this is substantially better than other old farmsteads that have been razed to the ground. On 13th December, 1986, the Dartmoor National Park Authority sent masons to undertake work on the doorway and windows of the front walls to protect against further decay.[22]

There is an interesting footnote to the history of John Bishop's House. In 1969, the BBC producer, John King, made a film called *The Stallion*. It is the story of a black Arab stallion who has escaped onto Dartmoor and runs wild. It takes advantage of mares belonging to a pony trader who lives on the moor, and who endeavours to catch the beast. The film was based on an idea by John King and the late David Rook, author of *The White Colt*. The cottage used as the pony trader's dwelling was John Bishop's House. John King said that a few repairs had to be made to the cottage, and Mrs Diana Coaker from Great Sherberton Farm elaborated further by telling how an asbestos roof and a new door were fitted. The effect was that it appeared as it must have once done while still lived in. John King also said that the actor who played the pony trader, the late Peter Arne, was at one time interested in leasing the property. This would indicate that the alterations to make the house into a shippen were fairly basic.

Peter Arne also insisted on doing all the riding required for filming, however dangerous. The stallion, Morfax, who starred in the film, came from Great Sherberton Farm and was owned by Annie Monro.

Hopefully, John Bishop's House will not be allowed to fall into total decay, but will continue to be maintained so that future generations can see where one of Dartmoor's best known dry-stone wall builders once lived.

Peter Arne with Morfax, during filming of The Stallion. © BBC

REFERENCES

1. Tor Royal Estate Sale Catalogue 1828
2. Parish Registers, Lydford
3. DCO(P) Estate Books
4. Crossing, W. *Crossing's Dartmoor Worker* David & Charles 1966 p35
5. *ibid.* p36
6. Parsons, H. Papers Unpublished MS n.d.
7. Crossing, W. *Amid Devonia's Alps* David & Charles 1974 p45
8. Hemery, E. *High Dartmoor* Robert Hale Ltd 1983 p366
9. DCO(B) Letters Received Book 1892
10. Crossing, W. *Crossing's Dartmoor Worker* p66
11. Hemery, E. op.cit. p366
12. Electoral Registers, Lydford
13. loc. cit.
14. Greeves, T. *Tin Mines and Miners of Dartmoor* Devon Books 1984 p2
15. Hemery, E. op. cit. p366
16. Electoral Registers, Lydford
17. PRO IR58/66261
18. loc. cit.
19. Electoral Registers, Lydford
20. loc. cit.
21. loc. cit.
22. *The Dartmoor Diary 1991* Devon Books and DNPA 1990

4. NUNS CROSS FARM

This chapter looks at the original Nuns Cross Farm only, as the second, more substantial building is still standing and, despite appearances, remains very much in use. The site of Nuns Cross Farm can be found at SX 605 698 and lies just over two miles south east of Princetown. Its height above sea level is 1280 ft (390m).

One of the last men to enclose a parcel of land on Dartmoor in the nineteenth century was John Thomas Hooper who, although originally from Withycombe Raleigh, had been living at Littleham near Exmouth.[1] He applied to the Duchy of Cornwall for a lease on 25 acres of unenclosed land in the vicinity of Nuns Cross, otherwise known as Sywards Cross, near Princetown. The actual bounds of the land applied for were "on or towards the West by the Forest boundary in that direction, on or towards the South and East by the Devonport Dock Leat, and on or towards the North by the said open Forest."[2]

The terms of the lease were for 31 years from 25th March 1870 and Hooper was to cultivate the lands and erect "a good substantial cottage with stone walls and slate roof".[3] The cottage was to be erected within two years from the date given. There was also to be a road put through the land not less than 20 feet (6.1m) in width. The rent was to be £2. 10s. per annum.

Crossing remembers the enclosing of the land, commenting that John Hooper "told me not long afterwards that by the time he had got up his walls and tiny dwelling, and bought a cow, his limited capital had disappeared, or, as his wife more forcibly put it, he possessed no more than 'fourpence hap'ny' to go on with."[4] Crossing also recalls being told that Hooper's wife (who incidentally was called Sarah) helped to build the farm walls. "Her part consisted more particularly of gathering stones and bringing them to her husband."[5]

While awaiting the completion of their new home, it would appear from the 1871 census returns that they lived in a make-shift structure nearby. Their address is given as "Hooper's Hut, Nuns Cross". Helen Harris also mentions a temporary shelter of "rocks and rushes" in her *Industrial Archaeology of Dartmoor*.

From early photographs of the farmhouse, it can be ascertained that it was a small, single storey, two-roomed dwelling. The roof, as the lease indicates, was not thatched but that of the attached outhouse was, as can be seen in the photograph. A nearby spring fed the pot-water leat bringing water to the house. The leat is now dry.

John and Sarah Hooper had two children, William and Anna Maria Staddon. The 1871 census returns give William's age as 20 and his occupation as an agricultural labourer, the same as his father, so it is likely he helped John on the little farm, rearing cattle. Anna Maria was 10 and would have attended school at Princetown.

Little is known of the Hooper's time at Nuns Cross Farm, but it can be assumed that John's venture met with success. Says Crossing, "During the later part of

The original Nuns Cross Farm with John Hooper and his dog. There is another figure to the left of the door. Note the hay rick, peat stack and knife grinder.

his life he was able to sell £100 worth of cattle yearly, which, considering the size of his place, was most satisfactory. But he worked hard, for though not a Dartmoor man born, he possessed all the instincts of one."[6]

Crossing also relates the story of how Mrs Hooper became lost on the moor in thick mist, arriving home at 4 o' clock in the morning. At 6 o' clock, two hours later, she set out to visit her son who was by then living at Loddiswell near Kingsbridge.

It would seem that Nuns Cross Farm did not occupy all of John Hooper's time as he found employment working for Mr Pearse, the farmer at Kingsett Farm in the parish of Walkhampton. Here, John would collect hayseed from the bottom of the cart and take it back to Nuns Cross Farm to improve the pasture there. His lunch regularly comprised a pig's ear which he would bring with him to Kingsett.[7] John is also reputed to have worked for a time at Whiteworks.[8]

Edward and Anna Worth. Anna was the daughter of John Hooper who built Nuns Cross Farm. Edward was one of the Peat Cot clan.

In November 1876, Anna Maria married Edward Worth, a general labourer and one of the Peat Cot clan. She began her married life at Peat Cot,[9] contrary to what has been claimed about their living with John and Sarah Hooper at Nuns Cross Farm.[10] They later moved to Whiteworks before settling into a house in Tavistock Road, Princetown. Edward's brother Isaac had married John Bishop's daughter Eden Ann in 1872.

John Hooper and his son-in-law Edward were employed in repairing the newtake walls of Fox Tor Farm in 1881, which had just been acquired by Mr James Lamb.[11] Hemery claims the repairing of these walls by John Hooper took place in 1901, but John had been long dead by this date.

Sarah Hooper died in April 1889, and it was presumably upon her death that John left Nuns Cross farmhouse and moved to Princetown to live with Edward and Anna and their large family of several children. He is recorded as a general labourer in the 1891 census returns and no doubt continued to work the land at Nuns Cross Farm. Edward is recorded as a Railway Packer. Six years later, in August 1895, John died aged 75. An obituary appeared in the local paper and gives an insight into his character:

"For the past 25 years, Hooper had been known to all lovers of Dartmoor. His weather-beaten features and unkempt locks betokened the character of the life he led. Amongst the solitudes of his surroundings, he was ever ready to guide the footsteps of a belated traveller, to cheer him with his hospitality, beguile him with the drollest of legends of Dartmoor, and, if necessary, walk a mile or two with him until he was set on the right tract. Outspoken, bold and fearless, Hooper will be sadly missed by antiquaries and others who looked upon Dartmoor as the 'lungs of Devonshire' and visit periodically the forest quarter."[12]

Anna and Edward Worth (lower centre) *and their sons. From left to right, top row:*
Arthur, Oliver, Thomas, Len, Harry, Sidney. Lower row: William, Anna, Edward, James.

Edward took over Nuns Cross Farm[13] and c. 1898, he converted it into a cattleshed, extending the property on the outhouse side. In 1901, Edward obtained permission from the Duchy to build the larger two-storey farmhouse that we see today[14] and, when built, he moved his family into the new three-bedroom house.

It is here that the history of the original farmstead ends. When it was also no longer required as a cattleshed, another of the nineteenth century farms was allowed to decay beyond repair. Today there is virtually nothing left except a pile of rubble and the odd piece of slate.

There is an interesting detail concerning part of John Hooper's land which is worth recording. In 1867, three years before Hooper acquired the lease, Reverend Daykin of Sheepstor leased a parcel of land in the area for the creation of Crane Hill Rabbit Warren, also known as Nuns Cross Warren. His boundaries were "on the North and East by a straight

Nuns Cross Farm, 1968. The original cottage is on the right.

line drawn from Nuns Cross to Plym Head and thence to Earme [sic] Head, on the South by a straight line drawn from the Earme Head to Plym Steps and on the West by the Forest Boundary to Nuns Cross aforesaid."[15]

Daykin employed Ditsworthy warreners, to act as his agents and run the warren. The poaching of his rabbits by local people was an occupational hazard; in 1872, John Creber of Longstone, Amos Creber of Nattor and John Legassick of Colleytown, all farms located in the parish of Sheepstor, were caught poaching. In 1876, a miner John Gould was similarly caught and sent to prison for 14 days.[16] Daykin eventually left Sheepstor and the lease was acquired by William Ware junior.[17]

The north and east boundary of this warren cut right across part of the land later leased to John Hooper. However, no problems with this for the Hoopers, Wares or Daykin have been documented.

Of the newer farm, its history lives on. After the Worths left, William Coaker and his family moved in (not Thomas as has been recorded elsewhere). They were followed by another Edward Worth, the Allen family and then the Phillips family. Although the Phillips lived and worked at the farm, it was actually leased from the Duchy by Mr A. Palmer of Walkhampton.[18] After the house had accommodated its last farming family, it became used by the Royal Navy as a base for adventure training. At the time of writing, the house is leased to Vernon White & Associates of Launceston, Cornwall. They run team development programmes for employees of computer and finance companies.

Perhaps this building will not suffer the same fate as other Dartmoor properties, but will be allowed to remain as a reminder of those hardy people who made a living from Dartmoor's unrelenting terrain.

REFERENCES

1. DCO(L) Box 35. Nuns Cross Farm docket. Doc: 23.3.1870
2. loc. cit.
3. loc. cit.
4. Crossing, W. *Crossing's Dartmoor Worker* David & Charles 1966 p.17
5. ibid. p.40
6. ibid. p.17
7. Greeves, T. (oral info. from Mrs. A.A. Matthews)
8. loc. cit.
9. Parish Registers, Princetown
10. Hemery, E. *High Dartmoor* Robert Hale Ltd 1983 p.338
11. DCO(L) Lamb's Tenancies docket. 1881
12. West Country Studies Library (Exeter) Newspaper Cuttings, Princetown
13. Electoral Registers, Lydford
14. DCO(B) Nuns Cross Farm docket. 11.1.1901
15. DCO(L) Box 25. Nuns Cross Warren docket. 30.8.1867
16. ibid. Newspaper Cutting 14.6.1876
17. ibid. Letter: 13.6.1888. A more detailed account of the history of this warren is given in *Dartmoor Magazine* 36, Autumn 1994 pp16-17
18. PRO MAF32/679/351

5. THE OCKERY

On the northern outskirts of Princetown, the B3212 road is carried over the River Blackabrook by Trena Bridge. Just a few yards downstream is Ockery Bridge, the clapper carrying the old packhorse track from Moretonhampstead to Plymouth. On the right of the river, at SX 595 741 is all that is left of Ockery Cottage; just a few visible foundations. It stands at a height of 1245 ft (380m) above sea level. Other spellings of The Ockery, as it is now called, are Okery, Okerry and Oakery, and the origins of this name are open to speculation. Perhaps oak timbers were used in the construction of the veranda surrounding the cottage, or perhaps it was named after the little grove of oak trees which can be seen downstream of the ruins.

The Ockery formed part of the Tor Royal Estate which was built on land leased from the Duchy of Cornwall in 1785 by Mr Thomas Tyrwhitt, Private Secretary to the Prince of Wales. During his life he was also auditor to the Duchy of Cornwall, member of Parliament for Okehampton and, later, for Plymouth, and Lord Warden of the Stannaries. He was knighted in 1812 when he became Gentleman Usher of the Black Rod. Tyrwhitt's purpose in leasing well over 2,000 acres in the area that was to become Princetown, was to establish a major agricultural estate. Apart from his Tor Royal house and associated buildings, other farms, cottages and establishments necessary to a growing community were constructed. He named this settlement Prince's Town after the Prince Regent and this evolved into Princetown.

Such was the climate on Dartmoor, and at Princetown in particular, that the long-term success of Tyrwhitt's agricultural dream never came to fruition, so he conceived the idea of housing Napoleonic prisoners of war in a specially built prison on his land. At the time, these prisoners of war were enduring the most appalling conditions while confined in hulks in the Hamoaze off Plymouth. The foundation stone of the prison was laid by Tyrwhitt on 20th March 1806. Thus the community developed around the prison and not agriculture. Tyrwhitt's life and involvement with Dartmoor have been well documented

The Ockery before renovation. Note the extension on the left.

elsewhere,[1] so suffice to say that, without him, Princetown would not exist.

The early 1800s witnessed a developing interest in Swiss culture, including that of architecture. Tyrwhitt's travels to the continent during this period may have been instrumental in his decision to build two of the houses on his estate, the Plume of Feathers Inn and The Ockery, in the Swiss style. Hamlyn Parsons maintained it was unlikely that Tyrwhitt was influenced by continental architecture, claiming that he did not go on the continent until 1813 (after the Plume of Feathers and The Ockery were built) when he took the Insignia of the Order of the Garter to the Tsar of Russia.[2] However, Tyrwhitt did go to Europe prior to this date; for example, in 1800 he went to Berlin.[3] To have developed an interest in the Swiss style does not necessarily imply that Tyrwhitt visited Switzerland as this type of cottage was also "common to the northern parts of the continent of Europe",[4] so he may have seen this style when travelling to Berlin.

The Plume of Feathers and The Ockery would have been forerunners of a fashion in architecture that was to sweep England after the Napoleonic Wars when the opportunity for continental travel became widely available once more. Ideally, a Swiss cottage should be built "in an undulating and always hilly country. The edge of a steep bank ... is very appropriate."[5] The Ockery, of course, was built on a bank but the Plume of Feathers is another matter. Indeed, concern was expressed by architects of the time that "there were really not many suitable settings for the Swiss Cottage in the relatively flat and rolling English countryside."[6]

Another Devon example of a Swiss cottage is the one at Endsleigh, built on the Duke of Bedford's Estate, and designed by Mr Jeffrey Wyattville, a favourite architect of the Prince Regent, with whom Tyrwhitt was in close association.

Originally, The Ockery was a small square cottage with a thatched roof, standing three storeys high.[7] The uppermost storey consisted of one large room under the roof where a window gave access to a view looking eastwards down the Blackabrook, which eventually flows into the West Dart. On the ground floor was a kitchen with stairs leading to the first floor, and another room, perhaps a bedroom. On the first floor were two bedrooms and a store cupboard.[8] The charm of the cottage lay in its exterior. It had been built of granite and the upper part was faced with hanging slates. A wooden veranda surrounded the cottage at first floor level giving it the 'Swiss chalet' look. The doorway to the veranda was situated in one of the bedrooms.[9] Access to the cottage was either by steps down from the road or through the gate next to the barn and over the clapper bridge. Although water from the river was in close proximity, a well was made and can still be seen in the front garden. The barn, once thatched, was built as a coach house and stable[10] but later became used as a turf house. [11]

The early years of The Ockery have been the subject of debate for over a century, and a popular date given for its construction is 1809, when it was supposedly built for the confinement of two French Generals on parole, Rochambeau and Boyer, who came to England as Napoleonic prisoners of war. However, as pointed out in Cecil Torr's *Small Talk at Wreyland*, Rochambeau was at Moretonhampstead from July 1807 to 1811 so, more recently, writers felt that their stay at The Ockery must have been prior to 1807.

In fact, at no time whatsoever did Rochambeau and Boyé (correct spelling) live at The Ockery on parole.[12] It is possible that they stayed here on the night of 2nd March 1811, on their way from Crediton and Moretonhampstead to Plymouth from where they sailed to Morlaix in France on the event of their repatriation. So the legend must at last be laid to rest.

Further research established that The Ockery was actually built c.1805. The earliest known record is for April 1805, when a lease was granted by the Duchy for a piece of land, and The Ockery was drawn in for reference. Records and other lease maps for the area before 1805 show no indication of a building here at all, despite Hemery's theory to the contrary.[13] The O.S. Surveyors Drawings of 1802-3 also show that no building existed here. The barn, on the left bank of the Blackabrook, was built between April and October 1808.[14] By September 1812, The Ockery had been extended and had a ground floor extension, which can be seen to the left of the photograph (page 68). This comprised one large room which, in the light of the accommodation required in future years, was probably divided into a kitchen/living area and a sleeping area. This was often achieved by the hanging of a heavy curtain across a room. It is possible that extra sleeping space existed under the roof. The extension formed separate, self-contained accommodation from the main cottage.

It is conceivable that The Ockery was built as a miller's cottage for Bachelor's Hall Mill, although later lived in by stonemasons and farm labourers, and that it is this cottage which was described as Bachelors Hall Mill Cottage in the 1841 census returns. Bachelor's Hall Mill, situated near the mine of the same name about half a mile downstream, was a corn or grist mill, providing flour for the local bakery run by Master baker, Richard Edwards, in his Plymouth Road premises.[15] The bread was then sold at the local market and also supplied to the prison. There is evidence of a wheelpit and leat on the site of the former mill.

Details concerning the earlier occupants of The Ockery have, to date, not come to light. Parish registers did not always give a precise address, merely stating "Princetown" under place of residence. It is not until 1822 that a definite name can be associated with the cottage. In the January of that year, labourer Richard Gerry of The Ockery and his wife Agnes had their son baptised in Princetown Church. As it was so early in the year, it would suggest the Gerrys were here in 1821 at least. Three years later, another son was also baptised, but the address is given as "Princetown", with Richard's occupation given as Miller, so it is uncertain whether, in 1825, The Ockery was still home to the Gerrys. They had definitely vacated the premises by 1829, and were living in the Slaughter House.

In 1828 Tyrwhitt sold the lease on his Tor Royal Estate, and it was bought by Mr George Nicholson.[16] Shortly afterwards, Captain William (Billy) Mitchell moved to the area from Lanteglos in Cornwall,[17] and on the Tithe Map schedule, he is listed as living at Bachelor's Hall. Two years later, the 1841 census returns show him and his wife Sarah, and a boy named William Lovey, living at "Bachelor's Hall Mill Cottage." It is possible that this is The Ockery, as suggested above, because there is no other reference which could be The Ockery in the returns.

From 1841 onwards, it becomes easier to trace the occupants of The Ockery, with fuller details emerging from the records. It is from this year that the name Kistle becomes associated with the cottage, and it was an association that was to span the duration of its remaining years. The census returns of 1841 show that James Kistle, a Cornishman aged 25, was living in Prison Barracks No. 3, with several other men. His occupation, as with the others, was that of stonemason, and they would have been employed at the nearby Fogintor Quarry. On 30th December, James married Eliza Austin, a tin miner's daughter, and from Duchy records it can be assumed they moved into The Ockery forthwith.

The extension to The Ockery meant that the cottage could accommodate more than one family, plus lodgers. In 1842, in addition to James and Eliza, were Joel and Ann Williams.[18] Joel was a stone cutter and probably worked with James at Fogintor Quarry. Sadly, in November 1842, Joel and Ann buried two of their children in Princetown churchyard; Selina aged 5 and John aged 3. They were to lose another daughter, Ann Selina, in 1852, while still at The Ockery. The Kistle's first child, Sarah Ann, was born in 1843.

The Tor Royal Estate was put up for sale in 1844. Sale particulars stated that "There is a very comfortable residence in the Swiss style called the 'Oakery' which affords every accommodation."[19] This further indicates that the cottage was well established for housing lodgers. The estate was sold to Mr Cholmondely Russell.[20]

The following year, the Kistle's second daughter, Jane, was born and in 1846, the baptism records show that a Walter and Mary Jane Treloar had moved into The Ockery and had their son, Walter baptised. Two years later they buried him. Walter Treloar was another stonemason, and stayed at The Ockery until shortly after his son's death.

The census returns for 1851 show that during this period, the cottage housed more people than at any other time during its history. The Kistles had produced four daughters, the two additional ones being Eliza Drucilla and Mary Ann. This family probably lived in the extension because the Williams' children had risen to five in number, and they also accommodated seven lodgers, so the extra space of the original house would have been very necessary. Five of the lodgers were stonemasons; Samuel Harvey, Thomas Connabeer, William Eva and Richard and Henry Collins. William Lambert was a gardener while Ann Laskey is listed as a widow. After 1852, there are no further references to the Williams family living at The Ockery. A Mary French lived here in 1859 and in the January, her illegitimate son, Charles Hazel was baptised.

James and Eliza Kistle, in the meantime, were adding to their family and by 1864 they had produced at least ten children, the remaining six being William James, Anna (or Hannah) Maria, Frederick, Thomas Henry, John and Edwin James. William died in 1863, aged 11 and Mary Ann died in 1870 aged 22.

By 1861, widower James Angel had moved into The Ockery with his son Emanuel, daughter-in-law Mary and niece Betsy Layman.[21] As a family smaller in number than the Kistles, whose five youngest children were still at home, they may have lived in the extension. James Angel was born in Buckfastleigh. He became a Sexton, and he and his wife occupied Crockern Cottage for a while, where they "used to attend to the wants of the clergymen who came to officiate at Princetown Church".[22]

James was also employed "for a while" at Tor Royal. His son Emanuel followed in his father's footsteps and became a Sexton.[23] But some of his working life, certainly while he was at The Ockery, was spent as a stonemason, an occupation common to the residents of this cottage.

The Kistle's third daughter, Eliza, brought another baby into the family in 1869, when she gave birth to an illegitimate son, William Glendower Bradshaw, whose father, Edward Hilton Glendower Bradshaw, is listed as a 'Gentleman' residing at Tor Royal.[24] The child only lived four years.

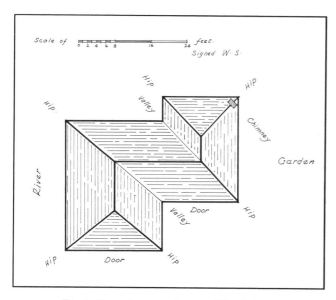

Fig. 1. Plans drawn up to re-roof The Ockery,
before the demolition of the extension, 1881.

Within the figure: Scale of ___ feet. 0 2 4 6 8 16 24 Signed W·S· — Hip — Valley — Hip — Hip — Chimney — Garden — River — Valley — Door — Hip — Hip — Door — Hip — Valley

The next family to join the Kistles were the Hannafords. The 1871 census returns show that Henry Hannaford, an agricultural labourer and his wife, Mary Anne, lived in the cottage with their ten month old son William. It is uncertain for how long they lived here, but by 1881 they had been replaced by tin miner Thomas Richards, his wife Hannah Maria (the Kistles' daughter) and their daughter Emily. Eliza Kistle, at the age of 63, is listed as laundress, and one of her sons, James (Edwin James), is a farm labourer.

There is not a great deal of documented information about the Kistles' life at The Ockery, or indeed about the other families and lodgers who lived here. James senior spent his working life as a stonemason, as did many of the other occupants, while Eliza brought up their many children, before taking up employment when they became independent.

As with other Dartmoor buildings, repairs to The Ockery were constantly needed, and in 1877, the roof was completely rethatched.[25] The cottage's lack of privy accommodation was also noted by the Duchy in 1875, and it is likely to have been then that one was built in the garden. By 1881 the cottage and barn were in a sorry state of repair, not helped by the recent storms that had swept the area.[26] Barrington recommended to the Duchy that the thatched roofs on both the cottage and barn be replaced with slate. Reed was both difficult and expensive to obtain, and that there was no thatcher within eight or ten miles of the place added further to the problem.[27] Barrington's recommendation was accepted in August 1881, and a plan of the proposed new roof for the cottage was drawn up (Fig.1). The following October, Mr Henry Caunter, a carpenter from Princetown, submitted an estimate of £18. 10s. for these repairs, while Mr William Stone of Chagford estimated a sum of £16.[28] In the event, repairs to the house, which proved to be more extensive than first thought, were postponed until the following summer. But those for the barn, then called the turf house, went ahead, the thatch being replaced with Coryton slate. Once finished, it was able to house three bullocks, and it also had a loft over.[29] The work was undertaken by both Caunter and Stone. In May 1882, they both submitted further estimates for the house repairs, the former's being £24. 12s and the latter's £36. Again, both men worked on the renovation,[30] and not James Kistle junior, as has been claimed.[31]

It was during the years 1882 and 1883 that The Ockery, which had remained unaltered from its Swiss style for over 75 years, underwent a complete change in character. These are the repairs which Brooking Rowe, Crossing and others discuss. Due to the irregular shape of the building, caused by the

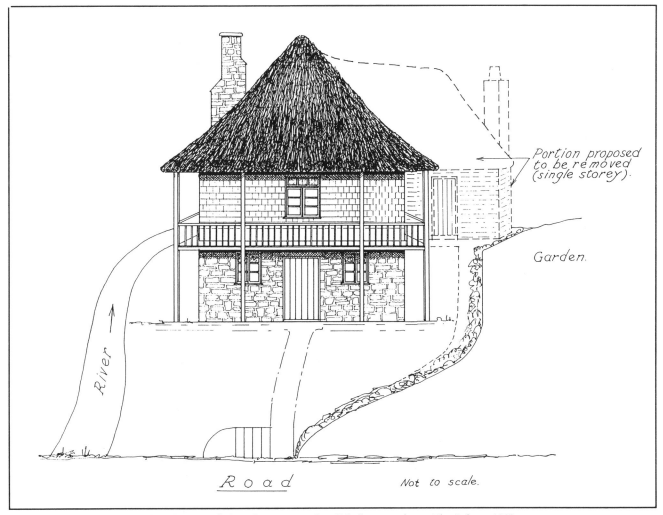

Portion proposed
to be removed
(single storey).

Garden.

River →

Road   Not to scale.

Fig. 2. *Copy of plans drawn up to demolish the extension to The Ockery, 1882.*

extension of c.1812, certain difficulties would have been encountered when replacing the thatched roof with slate. In the end, it was decided to demolish the extension, making the work involved much easier.[32] (Fig.2). After demolition, the foundations would have been apparent, and maybe it is these that made Hemery assume The Ockery had been built on the site of an older building.

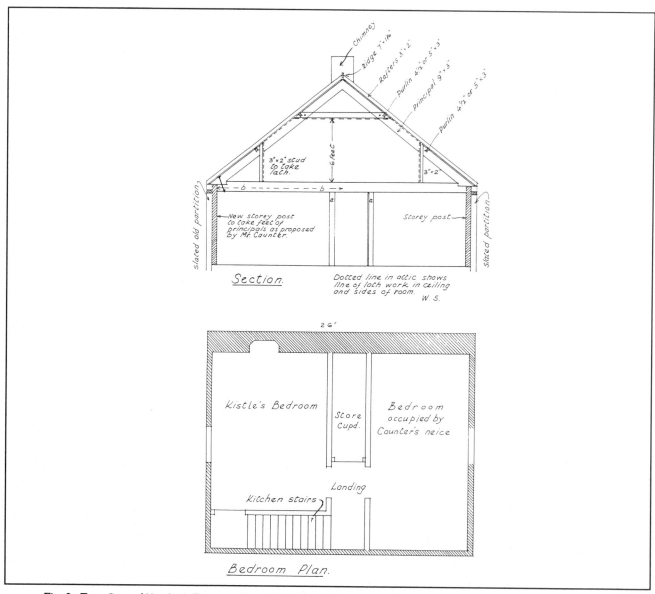

Chimney

Ridge 7"×1½"

Rafters 3"×2"

Purlin 4½" or 5"×3"

Principal 9"×3"

Purlin 4½" or 5"×3"

6 feet

3"×2" stud to take lath.

3"×2"

slated old partition

6 ——— 6

← New storey post to take feet of principals as proposed by Mr. Caunter.

Storey post

slated partition

Section.

Dotted line in attic shows line of lath work in ceiling and sides of room. W. S.

26'

Kistle's Bedroom

Store Cupd.

Bedroom occupied by Caunter's neice

Landing

Kitchen stairs

Bedroom Plan.

Fig. 3. Top: *Copy of 'Section'.* Bottom: *Copy of 'Bedroom Plan' - both drawn up for the alterations to the Ockery, 1882.*

Apart from the roof, other repairs included new joists, ceilings, floors, doors, window frames, down pipes and, of course, the removal of the veranda. A new ruling was introduced by the Duchy whereby all Duchy houses should have three bedrooms.[33] In all, the cost of the repairs was finally estimated to be about £80. The plans drawn up (Fig.3) indicate what was involved. It also shows that Caunter's niece was living with the Kistles. The third bedroom was under the roof.[34] The Hannafords by this time had left.

James Kistle senior had been unable to assist in the repairs due to his bad health, and he later died in 1886 aged 73, leaving his widow Eliza in the care of their son James. He occupied a "sitting room and bedrooms unfurnished"; a description appearing in the Electoral Registers for 1891, in which he is described as a lodger. The census returns for that year show that he was employed as a quarry worker. Also living in the house were Eliza's two grandchildren, Emily and Harry Richards. In his spare time, James

A postcard photograph of the renovated cottage c.1900.

Trena Bridge was widened in 1901 at around the time this postcard photograph was taken (what appears to be scaffolding stands by the bridge). The barn (right) was slate roofed in 1881, the cottage (hidden at left) was slate roofed a year later.

farmed The Ockery's four acre field and reared bullocks. He married his wife Clara during the early 1890s and started their family of eleven children. Some of these children's initials were inlaid into the garden path in different coloured cobblestones.[35]

In 1895, Mr Arthur Bellamy, who had been living at Powder Mills, moved into The Ockery with the Kistles and stayed for five years, returning to Powder Mills where he lived at Sunnyside.

Trena Bridge was widened in 1901 and it may have been that the stones which had been used as edging for the sides of the clapper bridge were used in the widening process.

On 3rd April 1904, James and Clara buried their daughter, Mabel Winnie aged just one month. It was not the only death to befall the family that year for on 19th November, Eliza Kistle died aged 85. At some stage before her death, she was removed from The Ockery to the Tavistock Workhouse, where she died.[36]

It would seem that the lease on The Ockery, which appears was now separate from Tor Royal, was not taken by James on his mother's death, but was acquired by Mr John Stroud, described as a resident of the cottage in the 1906 Electoral Registers. He also leased Prince Hall. By 1907, he had vacated The Ockery and was living in Caunter's Row in Princetown, although he did not relinquish the lease on the cottage until about 1908, and it was acquired by a Mr Perkins.[37]

Four years later, in November 1912, James died at the relatively young age of 48. Clara continued to run her late husband's small farming practice, as well as bringing up her large family of eight surviving children. This must have been a tremendous strain upon her and, tragically, she committed suicide in the May of 1914.[38]

It was during the early part of May 1914 that a neighbour, Mr Henry Caunter of Bachelor's Hall discovered that two of his pigs were missing, and after an extensive search of the area, he informed the Tavistock police.[39] One of the pigs was found in the barn at The Ockery, so a search warrant was issued on Tuesday 12th May, to make a search of the cottage itself. P.C. Weekes conducted the search but found no trace of the second pig. However, that afternoon, Clara visited Tavistock market where she tried to sell a portion of pig, which had obviously been too well hidden for P.C. Weekes. The following morning, she wrote a rather touching and poignant letter to Mr Coaker of Sherberton Farm.[40] It reads;

Dear Mr Coaker,

Will you be so kind as to come out as I am in great trouble. I have not a friend in the world, and have five children under 14 to keep. It is about Harry Caunter's pigs. I will give anything if you come out;
you told me you would any time I was in trouble.
C. Kistle. [signed]

P.S. Come out this morning.

But unfortunately, this was not to reach Mr Coaker; if it had, things might have been different. In the early hours of Tuesday 14th May, Clara was found dead in her bed by her thirteen-year-old daughter, Nellie.

An inquest into Clara's sudden demise was held at a cafe in Princetown, and the actual cause of death was not immediately apparent. Her struggles to rear her family single-handed, and the business of the pigs, were discussed at length, but it was felt she would not deliberately leave behind a young dependant family, and that she might have died of shock brought on by the police visit to her home. But searches of The Ockery after her death revealed a packet of arsenic, purchased in Tavistock. Thus an analysis of her stomach contents was deemed necessary, and this revealed that arsenic had been taken in sufficient quantity to cause death. The jury returned a verdict of "suicide while temporarily insane",[41] an undignified conclusion to poor Clara's life.

Because she had taken her own life, Clara was buried without burial rites in Princetown churchyard. She was laid to rest in the same grave as her late husband at 3p.m. on 19th May.[42]

The Kistle children, suddenly orphaned, were permitted by the Duchy to stay in the cottage, rent free until an uncle arranged for them to go into the workhouse or orphanage.[43] There is no record of them being admitted to Tavistock, so it is assumed they went to Plymouth. Unfortunately, the relevant records were destroyed in the Blitz during the Second World War.

The social history of The Ockery and its occupants ends on this rather sad note. It would seem the

Site of the Ockery today.

cottage was not lived in again. In 1915, an enquiry was made to the Duchy about the possibility of leasing the property but by then the cottage had fallen into considerable disrepair.[44] Hamlyn Parsons said that it stood derelict until about 1925, when it was demolished.[45] Thus another Dartmoor house and landmark disappeared. The barn was spared demolition and is still standing today.

REFERENCES

1. Crossing, W. *Princetown - Its Rise & Progress* Quay Publications (Brixham) 1989 and Gill, C. (Ed.) *Dartmoor: A New Study* David & Charles 1970
2. Parsons, H. Papers - Unpublished MS n.d. Westcountry Studies Library, Exeter
3. DCO(L) Box 57.
4. Lyall, S. *Dream Cottages* Robert Hale Ltd 1983 p.95
5. ibid. p.91
6. loc.cit.
7. DCO(L) Box 28. Letter: 19.5.1882
8. ibid. Plan 1882
9. loc. cit.
10. ibid. Letter: 10.10.1881
11. loc. cit.
12. Stanbrook, E. "A Dartmoor Legend: Two French Generals at The Ockery, Princetown" in *The Devon Historian* April 1991 pp.3-8
13. Hemery, E. *High Dartmoor* Robert Hale Ltd 1983 p.389
14. DCO(L) Lease maps: 30.4.1808 and Sept. 1812
15. Hemery, E. op. cit. pp.553-4
16. Crossing, W. op. cit. p.49
17. loc. cit.
18. Parish Registers, Princetown
19. Tor Royal Sale 1844 details. WDRO (Plymouth)
20. Crossing, W. op. cit. p.49
21. Census Returns, Lydford
22. Crossing, W. op. cit. p.37
23. loc. cit.
24. Parish Registers, Princetown
25. DCO(B) The Ockery docket. Doc.: 1877
26. DCO(L) Box 28. Letter: 16.6.1881
27. loc. cit.
28. ibid. Letters: 10.10.1881 and n.d.10.1881
29. PRO IR58/66261
30. DCO(L) Letters: 30.5.1818 and n.d.5.1882
31. Hemery, E. op. cit. p.389
32. DCO(L) op. cit. Letter: 19.5.1882
33. ibid. Letter:23.5.1882
34. PRO IR58/66261
35. Stephens, P. Oral info. given to David German
36. WDRO (Plymouth) Tavistock Workhouse Records
37. Electoral Registers, Lydford
38. *Totnes Times* 16.5.1914
39. loc. cit.
40. *Tavistock Gazette* 22.5.1914
41. loc. cit.
42. Parish Registers, Princetown
43. DCO(P) Letter to author: 1.10.93.
44. loc.cit.
45. Parsons, H. op. cit.

6. HUNTINGDON WARREN

Rabbit Farming

In the southern quarter of Dartmoor Forest at SX 665 669 and at 1430 ft (435m) above sea level, lie the ruins of the house and outbuildings associated with Huntingdon Warren. This was one of the last warrens to be formed on Dartmoor.

The first reference to Huntingdon can be found in the Lydford Court Rolls of 1479. The year before, William Bycote, from the parish of Buckfastleigh, took a horse belonging to Richard Yoland worth 2s. while it was at Huntingdon "lying between two Wellbrokes."[1] Bycote was presented at the Court for the offence the following year.

Rabbits are said to have been introduced to this country in the twelfth century by the Normans, but exactly when the farming of them started on Dartmoor is debatable. Writers often state that Trowlesworthy Warren on the River Plym was farming rabbits as early as the latter part of the thirteenth century. This was based on the supposed wording of the document in which Baldwin de Riparis (de Redvers) grants the tenement to Sampson de Traylesworthy (from whom the property presumably took its name). However, it would seem this is not the case. Recently, Jennifer Robertson has revealed there were no references to Trowlesworthy as a rabbit warren before 1651.[2] She feels that the assumption rabbits were farmed at Trowlesworthy in the thirteenth century comes from the editors of *Risdon's Chorographical Description or Survey of the County of Devon* who, writing in 1811, used the contemporary name of the property. In fact, it was never stated that Trowlesworthy was a warren at the time of the original grant.

To create a rabbit warren, natural boundaries formed by rivers were favoured, such as those on the Plym, otherwise boundary walls had to be constructed. The terrain on Dartmoor is not really suitable for an animal which needs to burrow, so artificial 'buries' or 'pillow mounds' had to be made. Basically, these were long, usually rectangular-shaped mounds of rocks covered over with soil and then turf to protect them from excessive rain. Each was surrounded by a drainage ditch. To further the drainage, buries were usually sited lengthways down a hill and drainage channels in the hills themselves were sometimes dug, as can be seen on Huntingdon Hill. Entrance holes were formed in each bury to allow the newly introduced rabbits ease of access to build their burrows and start breeding. The number of buries varies from warren to warren. According to R.G. Haynes, Huntingdon Warren has in the region of eighty, which is considered to be a high number.[3]

The breeding season was during the summer months and from September to March or April, they were caught by placing long nets over the buries while the rabbits were feeding on the surrounding pasture.

Huntingdon Warren pre 1949.

Dogs would be let loose and the rabbits would run for cover, straight into the waiting nets. After they had been killed and paunched (gutted) they would be sold at markets. Their skins would be returned to the warrener who would then sell them to the fashion trade. Ferrets and gin traps were also used.

The farming of rabbits attracted vermin such as stoats and weasels which had to be controlled, hence the vermin traps. These were stone-built contraptions, one large flat stone of about three or four feet in length being inserted into the ground to lie flush. A long stone would form one of the side walls while two smaller ones formed the other. This created a long tunnel-shaped space of a few inches in width down the

One of the many rabbit buries at Huntingdon Warren. The Wellabrook runs through the valley.

A vermin trap built into the inner western boundary wall at Huntingdon Warren.

centre, with an opening at each end and one between the two small side stones. The end openings had slate shutters which slotted into grooves, and the side opening accommodated the mechanism which dropped the shutters, and also another slate. The top of a trap was covered with a stone slab which spanned the trap to just inside the slates at each end, allowing them freedom of movement. Drilled into the cover stone were holes into which wooden poles were inserted. Fixed to these were thin wires which in turn were attached to the shutters. Funnel walls were usually built at both ends of the trap through which vermin would walk, and then on into the trap itself where the mechanism would be sprung, closing the shutters at each end and trapping the animal alive. Bait was rarely used.

The warrener then had the unenviable task of removing these 'vermin' from the traps and killing them, no doubt by breaking their necks or a swift blow to the head. Their skins would then be sold.
The use of vermin traps is thought to be pre-nineteenth century as it was then that the shotgun became widely used. Four vermin traps have been found at Huntingdon Warren, three in the boundary wall running parallel with the River Avon and one in the wall running parallel with the Western Wellabrook.[4] This last one is a doubtful example. As evidence suggests that no warren existed on Huntingdon Hill prior to the nineteenth century (see below), it implies that either a later date should be given to the demise of vermin traps or that the first warrener initially clung to old methods, perhaps using a shotgun as well.

With the shotgun came 'vermin houses' which were small stone constructions built near to where the vermin were known to breed and in which the warrener hid in order to shoot them on appearance.

Crossing mentions "little shelters, formerly used by the warreners"[5] on the southern slopes of Huntingdon Hill, built into three pounds. But they could have been lookout shelters instead, for the detection of poachers.

The Trist Connection 1722 - 1806

It has been well documented that Thomas Michelmore acquired the lease on Huntingdon Warren in 1809 and that he was the first of several generations of Michelmores to live and work at the warren. It was Crossing who repeated an unsubstantiated rumour, saying "it is said that a house and newtake existed there before 1700,"[6] which caused subsequent writers to make the same comment. However, Crossing gave no source whatsoever for this information, and despite recent searches through numerous documents, no evidence for this has been found. Instead, there is evidence to suggest that no house existed here before the close of the eighteenth century.

Until the early 1800s, the Duchy took little interest in its lands on Dartmoor or the tenants, as the area was seen as an unprofitable part of the estate. Consequently, tenants created newtakes through the manorial courts at Lydford without the knowledge of the Duchy. It was not until complaints were received by the Prince's Council that the Duchy introduced the granting of leases, mainly in the first few years of the nineteenth century.[7]

During this period of disinterest in Dartmoor on the part of the Duchy, the first newtakes were created on Huntingdon Hill, with the intention of assigning them to a wealthy Totnes man, Nicholas Trist. In 1722, the Court Rolls show that ten newtakes of eight acres each were formed by seven men; John Beard, Thomas Leaman, Richard Hext, John Hext, William Ellis,

William Willcocks and Richard Braker. At the same court, they were assigned to Trist at 12s. per newtake per annum. As some of this land incorporated old tinworkings, the overall total of land taken may have exceeded eighty acres.

Nicholas Trist was Lord of the Manor of Modbury, became Sheriff for the county of Devon in 1709 and was also M.P. for Totnes. He lived at Bowden House in Totnes with his wife Elizabeth (née Rooke), a Totnes girl, and their children. Nicholas owned several estates in the area including lands at Dean Prior and Ugborough, as well as leasing the lands on Huntingdon Hill which were tenanted by farmers for the grazing of stock. His eldest son, Browse, also enjoyed time as an M.P. for Totnes. On 6th June, 1734 he married Agnes Hore and they had nine children, one of whom became the Rev. Browse Trist. When Nicholas died in 1741, his eldest son Browse inherited his estates, and upon his death in 1777, the lands passed to the Rev. Browse Trist.[8]

At some stage, walls running alongside the Avon and the Wellabrook were built, probably before 1759 when the bounds of Huntingdon Tin Mine mention Huntingdon East Gate, which is very near Huntingdon Cross. One of the posts is still standing, albeit at a rather precarious angle. These walls may have marked the east and west bounds of the ten newtakes.

The Rev. Browse Trist married Elizabeth Wise and, of their three daughters, two survived, Elizabeth and Tryphena. On 13th December 1791, Rev. Trist died intestate, and from Duchy records it would appear that upon his death the eighty acres on Huntingdon Hill were then leased to his family with an additional parcel of "waste land" comprising 320 acres.[9] This must have been a rough estimate because the actual total of land on Huntingdon Hill held by the Trists at this stage was in fact 374 acres, 1 rood, 20 perches.[10] It may have been in 1791 that the inner north boundary wall was built, extending the eastern and western walls to the upper limits of land granted. The remains of a small structure can be seen in the north-east corner of this wall. This probably post-dates the house as there is no evidence of it on the O.S. Surveyors Drawings of 1802-3 or any other early document.

In the meantime, his daughter Elizabeth, while on a visit to Bath, had met and married a French Jew, Lewis John Marie Haussoulier, who was described as "one of the fortune hunters of the last century".[11] Hassoulier was under the impression that Elizabeth Trist was the daughter of a London gentleman and heiress to her father's estate of £40,000. So he married her. It was only afterwards that he discovered his fortunate mistake; he had married Miss Elizabeth Ashford Trist of Totnes who was heiress to an even greater fortune. In 1797, he became naturalised, and in 1799 "he assumed the name and Arms of Trist".[12] Elizabeth's marriage was not a happy one. When Rev. Trist died intestate, control of her father's estate passed to her. Her husband proceeded to squander much of the money. They had two children, a son and a daughter. The son died aged 6 months and Elizabeth died in 1799 when her daughter was only two years old.

It was after Elizabeth's death that a settlement document of 1799 was drawn up, making provisions for Browse's estates that had been in the care of his eldest daughter. It was ordered that after 22nd June 1799, all his estates should be "settled upon and vested in the said Tryphena Trist, her Heirs, Executors and Administrators".[13] It was recommended that the original 80 acres on Huntingdon Hill should be surrendered at the next Court Leet "for the time being", although it seems she was permitted to release them as she did not relinquish the land on Huntingdon Hill until 1806.

It appears likely that no house existed on Huntingdon Hill until c.1801-2. The 1786 Survey of Duchy lands[14] lists Browse's newtakes on Huntingdon Hill as land only. No tenement was recorded for either him or for anyone else in this area. The settlement document of 1799, which lists all Trist's lands and dwellings, gives no reference to a house on Huntingdon Hill either; again it is listed as land only. In May 1801, the land was put up for sale[15]. As it was in Trist ownership until 1806, it was either withdrawn from sale or it may have been sub-let. The sale particulars list it as land only - the 374 acres. It is probably now that Thomas Michelmore leased Huntingdon Hill from Trist and started to build the house and form the warren. Indeed, Carrie Waye, a descendant of Thomas Michelmore said that the Michelmores built the first house[16] (it burnt down in 1890 and had to be rebuilt). The 1802-3 O.S. Surveyors Drawing shows that only one building had been erected - no outbuildings as yet - and that the outer wall only of the home fields had been completed. The divisions had not been made.

Confusion about the date of the house was also caused by the tinners' mill on the western side of Huntingdon Hill near Broad Falls. Page referred to it as the ruins of an old warren house. Of this, Crossing said "I have recently noticed a statement to the effect that this old house was once the residence of a former warrener. This is incorrect, the present warren house, which is more than half a mile distant, is the original one"[17] - which of course confirms the statement made by Carrie Waye. Crossing too, says it was Thomas Michelmore (to whom he mistakenly refers as John) who formed Huntingdon Warren[18] and this has again been verified by Thomas' great-great-great- grandson,

Percy Waye, who confirmed that he built all the buries which were originally much higher than they are today, having sunk somewhat. It would therefore have been Thomas who made the vermin traps.

The Michelmores apparently came from Plymouth,[19] but before their occupation of Huntingdon Warren, they lived at Staverton until at least 1796, before moving to Buckfastleigh. Thomas had married Elizabeth Michelmore (a cousin?) at Buckfastleigh Church on 5th December 1785.[20]

In 1802 Trist's lease for Huntingdon Hill was renewed[21] and in 1806 Trist sold the lease to Thomas Michelmore.[22] On acquiring this, Michelmore asked the Duchy for a 99-year lease, to include an additional parcel of land.[23] He did eventually get this but not until 26th May 1809. The extra land increased the size of the warren to 585 acres, for which an annual rent of £4. 7s. 8d. was required. The bounds of the warren were now as follows: "abutting North on Fishlake Hill and Rider plain, North-east and East on West Wellabrook and Buckfastleigh Commons, South-east and South on Huntingdon Cross and the river Aven, and South-west and West on Pipers Beam."[24]

The boundary wall enclosing the new parcel of land on the north can be seen in both the field and on the O.S. Outdoor Leisure Map; the new western boundary can really only be seen on the map. The north easternmost boundary is now known as Higher Huntingdon Corner, and the north wall, described by Crossing as a "dyke and bank", crosses the upper part of T Girt.

This area formed an ideal site for a rabbit warren being bounded by rivers on all sides except the north, where the original wall and then the new "dyke and bank"[25] crossed the hill from one river to the other. The warren house was marked on the lease map of 1809, on the site of the ruins we see today.

The Michelmore Family's Occupation c.1800 - 1882

Thomas and Elizabeth Michelmore had ten children but not all survived into adulthood. Those who survived were John, William, Thomas, Elizabeth (Betsy) and Philip. One of their sons, either Thomas or Philip, went into service at Marley House as a butler for the Palk-Carews, and married Lady Carew's maid.[26] Marley House later became Syon Abbey.

The rabbit warren created by Michelmore is reputed to have been a thriving business, despite changes in agriculture where more emphasis was being placed upon growing winter fodder for livestock, resulting in increases in other forms of meat. As years passed, rabbit farming became less profitable due to the importing of different meats made possible by refrigeration on ships, a decline in demand for rabbit furs from the fashion trade, the 1891 blizzard when thousands of rabbits died, and myxomatosis introduced to Britain in 1954. This was followed by the rabbit clearance order of 1956. By then, Huntingdon Warren had ceased to be a rabbit farm.

During the Napoleonic Wars, the cultivation of corn and potatoes took place on various parts of Dartmoor, for example, at Hentor Warren, and were often grown down a hill rather than across it to ensure good drainage. Thomas Michelmore is known to have grown potatoes, and what are possible potato ridges can be seen on parts of Huntingdon Hill on the Wellabrook side. The two platts (small enclosed fields), which were built between 1809 and 1839, may have been used for potato cultivation especially as the larger one is indicated on the Tithe Map as an arable plot, though the lower one was then used for pasture. Hemery claims the smaller platt was a kennel court, as at Ditsworthy Warren, but there is no evidence of kennels here and, as well as the Tithe Map indicating otherwise, Percy Waye said his family had always used it for crops or pasture.

To protect the potatoes from frost after harvesting them, a potato cave was made and can be found to the west of the larger platt. This cave is now easy to find thanks to the two dry summers of 1989 and 1990. It had two granite posts on which a lintel was supported and a wooden gate was fixed across the entrance. Two good photographs appear in *Worth's Dartmoor*, one an exterior view, the other showing the interior. During the nineteenth century, the Huntingdon Mine owner was given permission to dig for tin inside the cave. Their searches came to nothing. This was probably in 1866 when John Parkinson was the mine owner. He informed the Duchy that the Michelmores had given permission for him to investigate the quality of the tin taken from an adit above the warren house.[27] Worth says, "the captain of the Huntingdon Mine saw in the [potato] cave the beginning of a possible exploratory drivage, and obtained consent from the tenant of the Warren for the continuation of the excavation into the hill. This carried the work deeper, to below saturation level, the cave was flooded, and so remains, thus its useful life was ended."[28]

Years later, young Percy Waye explored the cave which had dried out. He found well-preserved pick-axe marks and, at the end of the cave, he found two bats.

Michelmore's farming of rabbits on the southern moor was greatly appreciated by the workers employed in various ventures on Brent Moor, and later at Redlake. They would pay nocturnal visits to the warren lands and illicitly secure the meat needed for a tasty meal at no cost to themselves, "... labourers used to make incursions into Huntingdon Warren,

Former potato cave at Huntingdon Warren.

which is in full view from Western Whitaburrow, and trap the rabbits ... as many as a dozen being boiled at one time in the crock at the house on the cairn."[29]

So wrote Crossing who also complained that these men were responsible for destroying the old Petre's Cross. This poaching was not viewed in quite the same light by Michelmore, appreciation being far removed from his sentiments. He consequently built a small granite lookout shelter on the western slopes of Huntingdon Hill, just up from the tinners' mill near Broad Falls. This lookout blends into the hillside with its covering of foliage, and is not apparent until one comes across it. The internal measurements are approximately 42 inches by 108 inches (1.7m x 2.75m) and the walls stand about 39 inches (1m) high and are 22 inches (0.56m) thick. There is a chimney in the southern end, the internal measurements of which are 9 inches (0.23m) square. Inside the shelter, Thomas or a son would keep guard all night. If an all-night vigil was not possible, a light would be left burning or a fire smouldering to deter would-be poachers.[30] This shelter was still used in the days of Jan Waye, husband of Thomas' great-great-granddaughter,

Caroline Ann, earlier this century.[31] It is likely that another lookout was used on the other side of the Avon to protect the rabbits on that side of the river, but as one was not specially built, a tinners' hut may have been used.

The actual confrontation of a poacher (this time from Huntingdon Mine) and one of the Michelmore men is told by Crossing. In the series of articles written for the *Western Morning News* in 1905, and since published in book form,[32] he refers to the warrener who met the miner called Kit on the Lud Gate track. As the mine was working in the 1850s and 60s, it is likely the warrener in question was William, Thomas's son. The two men met at an upright stone, today known as Kit's Stone, named after the miner. Kit had taken advantage of Michelmore's absence from the warren and 'acquired' a couple of rabbits for himself. Michelmore, noticing Kit's bulging pockets, realised what had taken place.

"He, however, said nothing but began pitying Kit's poverty, and expressed himself at being sorry that he had no better clothes than the rags he was wearing. At length he vowed Kit should have his coat, which was a good one, and said that he would make shift with the miner's. Kit, who saw the warrener's drift, pretended to be very reluctant to deprive him of his garment, but while talking, contrived to push the rabbits which he had in his pockets, through the torn lining, inside the waist-band of his capacious corduroy breeches. Then pretending to yield, he took off his coat, but would not give it up until the warrener had handed his over to him. Having received it, Kit put it on, and quietly walked off. The next morning, the warrener approached him, while at his work. 'I was deceived last night', he said; 'I ought not to have changed coats.' "Aw ees, that was

all right", replied Kit, 'if you'd aunly a volley'd it up. You auft to ha' changed another garment too.'"[33]

Huntingdon Warren house was a two-storey building with three rooms on each floor,[34] so accommodation was not as cramped here as in other farmsteads. The roof was thatched and remained so until 1890, when slate was substituted, and the house slightly enlarged. There were various outbuildings near the house for a few cows, pigs and poultry. There was also a domestic garden, where a search will reveal steps. Flowers grew and in the spring daffodils still appear.

The look-out hut on the western slopes of Huntingdon Hill, used by the warreners to watch for poachers.

The water supply came from a well which was dug near to the house. At some stage it became covered over and water was obtained from another well at the site of a spring in a nearby field. The Tithe Map shows this in one of the home fields which was called 'Well Park'. The well near the house was not uncovered and used again until early this century.[35]

In 1815, Thomas Michelmore mortgaged Huntingdon Warren to John Fox Smart to secure the sum of £250 plus interest, which was paid off during the next few years.[36] In the 1830s, Thomas retired from his work as warrener and let his two eldest sons, John and William, run the business. He and Elizabeth remained at the warren house, living in one room.[37] In November 1840, at the age of 82, Thomas died and was buried at Buckfastleigh. He left the warren to John and William who, in 1841, together with John Fox Smart, again mortgaged the property, this time to Robert Tucker and John Prestwood Bellow, to secure £300 plus interest.[38]

John and William continued to run Huntingdon Warren successfully. Their sister, Elizabeth, died in 1845 while their mother died in 1850, aged 86. The 1851 census returns show that the house was occupied by John, William, their brother Thomas and a Mary Ann Can. Thomas and Mary Ann are described as servants. Philip Michelmore had married Ann Coombes in 1827 and was working as a woolcomber in Buckfastleigh, where he, Mary Ann and his daughter lived. Philip's two sons, William and Philip, had left home and William was working as a woolcomber too. He had married Amelia, and the first of their children had just been born. It was this branch of the family that was to carry on the line of Michelmores at the warren.

During this period, relations between the Michelmores and the Huntingdon Tin Mine owners became strained. The mine had re-opened in 1851 as Avon Consols. In June 1852, a new leat was being cut to the mine through the lands of Huntingdon Warren, much to the annoyance of the Michelmore brothers who deliberately interfered with the flow, resulting in a loss of working days at the mine.[39] Their solicitor insisted that unless an agreement could be reached between the mine owners (Christopher Robins and William Pearse) and the Michelmores, the leat would have to be filled in. The Michelmores were demanding £10 damages and £5 rent, whereas Robins was only prepared to pay £1 and 2s. 6d. respectively; a slight difference! This dispute continued into the July and mining operations had to be suspended.[40] The matter was eventually resolved, although records do not elaborate. However, twelve years later, the Michelmore brothers again demanded damages of £19. 10s. 3d. for the leat,[41] and again, in 1866, when John Parkinson had taken over the mine, there was trouble. The Michelmores had threatened to cut off the water supply to the mine unless Parkinson paid them money for attending to the mine after it was purchased by him. So in all, there appears to have been a continuous degree of acrimony between the parties. As Duchy records show, "the Tenants have always been opposed more or less to Mining within the Warren, on the grounds that considerable damage is done from time to time by the Water overflowing the Banks of the Leat, and thereby destroying the Rabbits especially in the breeding season."[42]

Despite the various disputes between Parkinson and the Michelmores, it appears that William Michelmore did actually do some work on the mine. In 1868 he took Parkinson to court in Totnes for failing to pay him for labour done on the sett. In the July, Michelmore complained to the Duchy that, despite the court case, Parkinson had still not paid him.[43]

If one follows the leat around Huntingdon Hill to the Avon, small granite bridges can be seen spanning the leat, put over for the convenience of rabbits and warreners. On the leat above Huntingdon clapper bridge (built by Thomas Michelmore) is another wide clapper bridge that must have been made to accommodate a horse and cart. A ford at Bush Meads was the crossing place over the Avon for a horse and cart.

Both John and William remained single until sometime in the 1850s, when John married and went to live with his wife in Fore Street, Buckfastleigh. He

Huntingdon Clapper spanning the River Avon.

appears to have married the Mary Ann Can who appeared in the 1851 census returns. It was probably upon John's marriage and subsequent removal from the warren house that Philip's elder son, William, and his family moved in. Philip died while at Christow in 1857 and, as neither John nor William had any children, William junior took over the rabbit farming, selling the rabbits "in Totnes, Chudleigh, Newton Abbot and the former Friday meat-markets in South Brent, transporting them thither by packhorse."[44] John and William Michelmore retained an active interest in the warren until their deaths, both occurring in 1868.

In 1861, William Michelmore junior applied to the Duchy to rent a tract of land adjoining Huntingdon Warren in the area of Buckland Ford and the Western Wellabrook, at an annual rent of £1. He intended to enclose the land with a turf ditch but not cause any damage to the Abbots' Way.[45] This additional parcel of land is likely to have been what brought the acreage of the warren up to 609 acres, a figure often erroneously attributed to the 1809 lease. This land was needed by Michelmore to enable him to deal with the poachers shooting his rabbits.[46]

After 1862, rabbits were no longer protected and were classified as game. This resulted in many farmers in Britain breeding rabbits as a sideline which in turn affected warreners' trade. The Michelmores' trade was affected too, no doubt .

In 1865, John and William again mortgaged Huntingdon Warren to Robert Tucker for £300 plus interest, to be paid off by their nephew William. The money obtained from this mortgage was to secure 10s. a week for the rest of John's life and if he died before his wife, she was to receive 5s. a week until her death. If William senior was to outlive John, he was to be kept in board, lodging and clothing until his demise. Then Robert Tucker would possess the property for the remainder of the term agreed, upon trust for William junior. By 1882, 14 years after John's and William's deaths, the mortgage had been paid off.[47]

William and Amelia had a large family of at least eight children, and Philip's widow, Ann, also lived with them for a while. Their son, William Henry, was employed at Huntingdon Mine where he was in charge of the horse at the horse whim.[48] It was about this time, in 1870, that his father was demanding compensation from the China Clay Company for cutting a new leat through the warren lands on the right bank of the Avon. It is the cutting of this leat to which Crossing refers in his *Amid Devonia's Alps*, and which was still in the process of being made in 1871. "I here showed George a small wooden aqueduct - or launder as such is locally termed - erected to convey water across this gully, and which I had seen in the course of construction in the summer of the previous year [ie. 1871]. This water was taken in from the Avon close at hand, and conveyed along the sides of the hills, to the clay pits on Brent Moor, for the purpose of washing the clay down to the works at Shipley."[49]

Also, in the December of 1871, Michelmore decided he wanted the rights to work a sett running through his lands for himself,[50] maybe in the area of the potato cave. This did not please Mr J.H. Bennet who had an interest in the mine workings. Michelmore had told Bennet's father of the tin lode passing through the warren and that he had obtained permission from the Duchy to sink costean pits etc. on the back of the lode. If all seemed satisfactory, Michelmore could then apply for a grant to work the sett. Bennet did not approve of this or the fact that another party had made an application to work the sett, and he asked the Duchy to intercede.[51] The outcome is not known but there were no more references to Michelmore working a sett in the records.

Living out on the moor did not suit all the Michelmores. Percy Waye recalled how his great uncle Charlie, William and Amelia's son, walked back home to the warren house one evening in torrential rain, getting his new suit absolutely soaked and mud splattered. As a consequence, he packed his bags and left the next day, saying he would never return there to live. Instead he went to live at Holne where he became the village thatcher.[52]

In 1880, William was considering vacating Huntingdon Warren, which by now he was working with two of his sons, William Henry and Richard James. This prospect interested William Ware of Ditsworthy Warren in the Plym valley, who knew of a potential lessee, but this came to nothing.[53] A few months later, in 1881, interest in the property was expressed by magistrate Edmund Fearnley Tanner of Hawson Court near Buckfastleigh. Tanner's interest stemmed from his involvement with local hunts. He had been Master of the South Devon Hunt for the

1878-9 season but had received little support so he resigned from this to hunt his own pack. One of his pack's runs was from Huntingdon Warren to Fox Tor and Rippon Tor. The use of Huntingdon Warren would have been ideal because an area with plenty of rabbits means an area with no shortage of foxes. As the Rev. W.H. Thornton said, "the rabbit trapper with his gin is a deadly enemy to the fox, and the game preservers are not always very friendly."[54]

Warreners had to shoot foxes to protect their rabbits, but Michelmore was paid £20 per annum by the Dartmoor Hunt not to do so.[55] The areas over which Tanner ran his hunt were Buckfastleigh, Fox Tor, Princetown, Cator, Rippon Tor and Avon country.[56] He kept his hounds in kennels at Hawson Court.

Tanner's Occupation 1882 - 1908

Tanner was intent on acquiring the lease on Huntingdon Warren and expressed fears that other people had been negotiating for it.[57] The property itself was in a very run-down state with very few rabbits and the house needed some attention. The Duchy said that if he was seriously interested in the lease, he must agree to undertake the responsibility of fencing all the enclosures and keeping the house well maintained.[58] Tanner was agreeable to this and so, in 1882, the lease passed out of the Michelmore family. However, Michelmore did retain 91 acres of land to the south-west, where he kept a mare and colt. He now lived at Runnaford (some records say Bunnaford) Coombe near Buckfastleigh.

On 4th September 1882, during the Forest Drift, both Michelmore's mare and colt were driven away and impounded by the moormen, a demand of £1. 6s. being made for their release, which he had no choice but to pay.[59]

Carrie Michelmore (right), Millie Michelmore (left) and their grandmother, Amelia Michelmore b. 1828. A photograph taken at Hele, Ashburton.

Mr E. Fearnley Tanner.

Michelmore's retention of this land was to be the cause of great tribulation to Tanner. Writing to the Duchy in November 1882, he complained that Michelmore was trying to catch his rabbits "and I have had to remove all the rabbits that side to save their lives and my pocket".[60]

About three weeks later, the Duchy commented that "... as long as Mr Michelmore is in possession of the land in question it is in his power to cause considerable annoyance to Mr Tanner ... and as the parties do not appear to be on very good terms it is quite possible that Mr Michelmore will take advantage of his position to do so."[61]

Four years later Michelmore was still in possession of this piece of land. In the April, he and two of his sons and a Farmer Horton were accused of night poaching at Huntingdon Warren; it seemed that warrener had now turned poacher. A Court Summons was issued causing Michelmore much fury, claiming he was afraid of Tanner and that he and his sons had not been near the warren for a year. He accused Tanner and his men of making false statements about him, and that he would now consider vacating the land. Despite his protestations, the four men went to court, were convicted and fined. Horton decided to take the matter to the Exeter Sessions, but an out-of-court agreement was settled with Tanner instead. Tanner refused to do the same for the Michelmores[62] and no doubt they paid the fines levied by the court. Michelmore quit the land at Lady Day 1887, and so the entire Huntingdon Warren lands were now in the possession of Tanner. William Henry Michelmore moved to Poundsgate about this time where he ran the local shop.

Tanner himself did not live at the warren house but sub-let it to various tenants. Between 1882 and 1885 the tenants were Messrs Fortescue and Broad respectively.[63] In 1886 Mr Broad left and James Stancombe and his family moved in, his children Edith and Ernest attending Coombe School, near Scorriton.[64] Crossing mentions Fortescue and Broad but the dates he gives for their occupation of the warren are inaccurate.

To ensure easier riding over the mires at Fishlake and Heng Lake, Tanner made a stone causeway and it became known as 'Tanner's Path'. It is no longer in use today and is virtually untraceable. It has been claimed that Tanner made this causeway after World War One with Jan Waye, but this seems unlikely as Tanner went to live in Winchester in 1906[65] and had relinquished the lease in 1908, four years before Jan Waye moved to the warren.

In 1887, Tanner gave up the Foxhounds, having broken his jaw the previous year, but he still retained the lease on Huntingdon Warren and let it to the Dartmoor Hunt. In 1889, Mr Hubert Harris de Burgh moved into the warren house with James Stancombe, and the following year, on 24th January 1890, the house was completely destroyed by fire, and with it, all Mr Harris's furniture and effects.[66] Only the stone walls were left standing, "and they are much

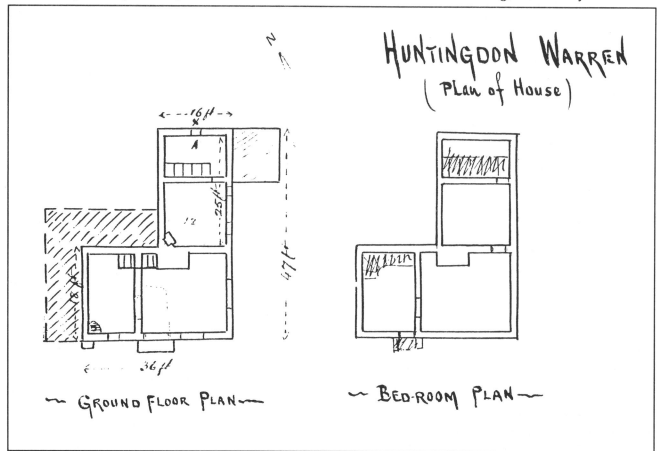

Fig 1. *The plan drawn up by Mr Tanner in 1890 for a replacement building at Huntingdon Warren. The original one burnt down in that year.*

damaged."[67] Mr Harris was compelled to live in a wooden hut, erected nearby. It would seem that Stancombe was absent during the period of the fire and its aftermath as Duchy records do not indicate that his possessions were also lost.

The Duchy decided to rebuild the house, taking the opportunity of improving on the original model. Tanner had had the foresight to insure the property, so they would only have to pay for the extra requirements. Tanner himself drew up the plans for the reconstruction, shown in Fig.1, and he planned to use his own men to undertake the work. He intended building the house more or less as it had been but with a few amendments. He wanted to substitute "Swedish timber for rough slabs, slates for thatch, stout glass windows for scraps, and making the room marked A which is a store with no light into a dwelling room with window, lath and plaster, and a bedroom up over also lath and plaster, building a gable on the end X. To do all this, the walls must be heightened 2ft all round."[68]

The estimated cost was £34, of which Tanner was prepared to pay £10, the Duchy paying the balance.

The men in Tanner's employ began clearing the site on 17th February, and completion of the building was the following September,[69] when the tenants were able to move back in. By early 1891, brothers John and Ronald Harris de Burgh had moved into the warren house together with Aaron and Elizabeth East, their gardener and housekeeper. James Stancombe seems to have continued his association with the warren but no longer lived there.[70] Crossing implies a Mr Harris [de Burgh] was here until 1903 but in fact, in 1895, John Hannaford moved to the warren, his children attending Coombe School. By 1901, William (Fred) and Beatrice Pearce and their children had become occupants of the warren house, their children too,

being educated at Coombe. It is William Pearce to whom Crossing refers in his *Guide to Dartmoor* as the late warrener of Huntingdon Warren. Hemery claims Crossing was mistaken and that Pearce was Thomas Michelmore's 'man', but this is incorrect. It was Pearce who put a plank across the Avon as a means of crossing the river when the clapper partially collapsed after a flood. This was superseded by a more substantial timber bridge at Broad Falls, put up to give easy access for the workers at Redlake.

Mrs Pearce supplied the Martin brothers with some of their provisions during their annual camping holidays on Dartmoor. In 1904, Arthur, Jack and Keble Martin, together with their Champernowne cousins and some friends, began their first summer holiday of many camping by the Western Wellabrook near the warren house. These camps were to continue until at least 1913.[71] The Martin brothers were the sons of the Rev. Martin of Dartington, and Jack and Keble were to follow in his footsteps and make a career in the church. Keble also developed a very keen interest in botany and later wrote the well-known book *The Concise British Flora*.

The Martins rode their bicycles from Dartington to Hayford Hall where they were permitted to leave them, before walking out to their camping site.[72] Food was never in short supply, being supplied by the Parsonage kitchen, and grocer, Mr Tucker of Totnes. Mrs Pearce supplied them with eggs, milk, bread and the occasional rabbit pie. According to Keble Martin's autobiography, postal deliveries were daily.

By the time their camping holidays began, Jack and Keble Martin had made their commitment to the church so when, in 1905, a child at Huntingdon Warren was to be christened, they were able to perform the ceremony. On 2nd August, Jack, who was the Curate at Dartington, conducted the christening ceremony of Vera Millicent Pearce at the warren house. This ceremony was then registered in the Buckfastleigh and Princetown parish registers. It has been said that this was also done for Lydford, but no record of this has been found in the parish registers.

What is today known as 'Keble Martin's Chapel' or 'Matins Corner' was formed in 1909. "It consisted of rough paving on the floor of the dell, then a flight of three solid granite steps with flanking boulders up to a small grass terrace and a granite pier with a cross on it, incised in the granite by Arthur with Jack's cold chisel and hammer."[73] This little 'chapel' is still in evidence today, as is Arthur's cross and the 'Chi-Rho' symbol on one of the steps.

Mr Cottier, China Clay Companies and the Return of the Michelmores 1908 - 1940s

In 1908, Tanner gave up the lease on Huntingdon Warren; he had, in 1906, moved to Winchester. The lease was then sold to Mr Charles Edward Cottier of Plymouth, and Mr C.J. Payne. Cottier also acquired the lease for Redlake, Harford and Ugborough Moors. Cottier had in fact approached the Duchy regarding mineral rights in the Redlake area in 1904, and in 1905, he sent a mineralogist to the area to search for china clay.[74] This was Richard Hansford Worth, who found clay deposits at Redlake, although it was later maintained that these deposits had been found by Ned Bray and Jack Hooper.[75]

The surface lease for Huntingdon Warren was dated 25th March 1908, and was for a term of 30 years and 129 days at an annual rent of £25.[76] Two years later, Cottier formed the China Clay Corporation Limited, whose headquarters were in Ivybridge. The leases of 1908 were then acquired by the Company on 7th March 1910. Although there was a change in lessee, it would seem that the Pearces stayed until 1909, when they went to Bickington. Between 1909 and 1912, Mr and Mrs Willcocks and their sons, Leonard, Albert and Samuel, lived here. They moved to the warren from Sparkwell.[77]

There is an interesting description of the warren house for this period. "Stone built cottage with slate roof. Walls partly plastered partly covered with corrugated iron sheeting. Small shed for cows poor condn stone built with thatched roof. E.C. [? Earth Closet] in field iron built. 2 small sheds iron roofed. The Dwelling house contains par. [parlour], kit., Bk kit [Back kitchen], pantry & 4 bedrooms."[78]

In 1912 the Michelmore family returned to Huntingdon Warren. Thomas Michelmore's great-great-granddaughter, Caroline Ann, daughter of William Henry who had gone to live at Poundsgate, married John Waye c.1911, and they moved into the warren house the following year with their baby son, Percy, as tenants of the China Clay Corporation Ltd. John had been a coachman, and Caroline a cook at Hele, Ashburton,[79] and when they married, they initially went to live at Warmacombe.

John Waye (known as Jan) worked at the warren farming rabbits and other livestock until 1917, when he was called up for service in World War One.[80] His wife, Caroline (known as Carrie), decided to move to her parents home at Poundsgate, from where young Percy went to Leusdon School. His sister, Stella, was born at Poundsgate in 1918. Instead of leaving the warren standing empty until Jan Waye's return, William and Rosina Coaker moved in and ran the place. When Jan returned from war, he and his family

Members of the Waye family with visitors beside the River Avon. c.1920s (early). Top second left to right: *Percy Waye and dog, Stella Waye and John (Jan Waye).*

returned to the warren, the Coakers staying on until 1920.[81]

After the war years, life at the warren resumed for the Wayes, with income from the rearing and selling of rabbits being supplemented by other means, partly due to stiff competition from the Plym warrens and Headland Warren, and the declining prices now being offered for dead rabbits. Jan therefore found employment at Redlake and Leftlake, where he looked after the horses, initially taking his own cart-horse to the workings each day.[82]

By the end of World War One, the China Clay Corporation was in difficulty largely due to shortages of labour, and the company collapsed in 1919. It was put up for auction on 20th October 1920 with a reserve price of £200,000, although it was hoped to realise double that amount. Hopes were dashed. Bidding stopped at £47,000. It was, by order of the court, sold for this sum to the bidder in question, Mr Harry Mallaby Deeley.[83] He named his new company the Ivybridge China Clay Company Limited. It was after the former company was eventually wound up that Jan Waye was able to acquire the lease on Huntingdon Warren - probably from Lady Day 1924.

In November 1927, tragedy struck the Redlake community. A seven-year-old boy of one of the workers, called Ivor Gordon Thompson, was playing football with sixteen-year-old Russell Heath. Thick

John Waye (lower right) *working at Redlake.*

Huntingdon Warren house c.1930.

mist descended and Ivor became lost. His body was found the following morning on the bank of one of the Erme's tributaries. Of the many wreaths at his funeral was one from "Mr and Mrs Waye and all at Huntingdon Warren."[84] The Redlake workers decided to erect a cross in the boy's memory, on the spot where he was found, but this seems never to have happened.

The new Ivybridge China Clay Company was not to survive long. The Great Depression that was affecting the whole of Britain during the 1920s and 30s was also felt by the mining industry in Devon. By 1932, output from both Redlake and Leftlake had fallen dramatically, and in this year, both workings closed.

Before the demise of this company, Mrs Waye and her children used to travel by locomotive to Cantrell where the track ended at a siding. From here, they would go to Ivybridge, catching a locomotive back up to Redlake at the end of their trip - outings Percy Waye remembers well. In his book *The Redlake Tramway*, E.A. Wade says that the warrener's daughters would travel on the locomotive to the southern extremity on a Monday morning and then walk into Ugborough where they attended school. They would stay with friends in the village during the week, returning to Huntingdon Warren on the Friday. In discussion, Mr Wade feels he was given inaccurate information. It certainly does not correspond with any other sources. Huntingdon Warren children appear to have attended the schools at Coombe and Holne only.[85]

With the collapse of Mallaby Deeley's Company, Jan Waye had to find other ways of making a living, so he developed his interest in livestock, rearing Galloway cattle, Blackfaced sheep, pigs, chickens, ducks, geese, guinea fowl and turkeys. Crops grown in the two platts were cabbages, swedes, 'flat-polls', and potatoes. One year they tried growing corn. During the summer months, they also took in visitors, guests including Keble Martin and Richard Hansford Worth, and also Mr Symes to whom the warren house was later sub-let. Sometimes Carrie Waye would have to cook for as many as nine people. Another visitor was Marjory Eckett Fielden, who recalled the following incident.

"Staying out at Huntingdon Warren in the autumn of 1935, at 8.30 a.m. one day I let out the geese as it was my daily treat to do, but on going to feed them at 9 a.m. I found that they had mysteriously vanished!

The son of the house, on arriving at about 11 o' clock that morning at the Stroll, by Warnacombe [sic], two and a half miles away 'in over', found the geese happily making themselves at home in their former quarters.

Although they had been taken out to the Warren a few days before in hampers on a cart, old Gander, by some marvellous instinct, had unerringly led his little party back over the moor to the home of his choice."[86]

The farming of rabbits continued at the warren until the early 1930s. With Jan busy at Redlake until 1932, the services of trappers were employed, one being Mr Diamond.[87] They would stay for three to four weeks before moving onto another warren. The trapping of rabbits in the Waye's time was often done using ferrets and net but gins were used too. The setting of these would require a morning's work, followed by regular checks to remove and kill those caught in them. Stella Waye recalled that as a child, she felt sorry for these rabbits, so one day she went round every bury letting off all the gins she could find. Unfortunately, she caught two of her fingers in one of the gins and had to enlist her mother's help to be set free. The trapper was far from pleased![88] Once killed, the rabbits would be paunched and a slit cut in one back leg through which the other back leg would be pushed. The rabbits would then be arranged in a hamper with a pole across the centre over which the rabbits would be hung. Once the hamper was full, the trapper would take it back to the warren house, and Jan Waye would take them by horse and cart to Buckfastleigh Station from where they would be sent to various towns including London. For each rabbit, Jan received 6d. and the trapper was paid 3d. After taking the rabbits to the station, Jan would go into

Buckfastleigh town for shopping and refreshment at one of the hostelries. Occasionally, Carrie and the children would go too.

The rent for Huntingdon Warren was paid once a year at the Duchy Hotel in Princetown, where all Duchy tenants would be given a dinner and churchwarden pipes. Jan would travel to Princetown on horseback via Tanner's Path, Fishlake Gully and Black Lane. After the evening's entertainment, he would return across the moor, not reaching home until 3 or 4 o' clock in the morning.[89]

Percy and Stella went to school at Holne and then Coombe, riding out there on their white horse called Bobby. They would leave home before 8 o' clock, meeting the Redlake workers from the Scorriton area on their way. The horse would be left with their Uncle Charlie Michelmore at Higher Coombe and, on reaching school, Stella would sometimes be given a

Carrie Waye with Stella on Bobby the horse. Stella is holding a white cat.

saucer of tea to freshen her up.[90] There were no school dinners so Percy and Stella would take homemade pasties or ham sandwiches. School ended at about 4 o'clock and then there was the long ride home again. Usually Carrie had their tea ready for them, but one day she was delayed on the moor while rounding up the livestock, and the two children came home to an empty and dark house. Stella began to cry, so Percy found her a piece of paper and a pencil and told her to draw a cat![91] For some of the time, the children would stay in Holne with a relative during the school week, going home for weekends.

On the path leading from Lud Gate to the warren house, there are various distinctive stones which Percy and Stella named. After reaching the two thorn trees that are visible on the brow of the hill, and passing Kit's Stone mentioned above, there was 'Granfer's Stone', a flat rock on which their grandfather sat the last time he ever visited them. On from that was 'Little Man' which has since disappeared.

Peat was still the main source of fuel and the peat tie was up near Huntingdon Barrow, otherwise known as the Heap o' Sinners. The peat would be cut using a slitting knife, budding iron and turf iron. When cut, it would be moved to a drier area on a sledge or 'slide' where it was stacked to dry, being turned over after a few days. When dry, the slabs of peat would be put on to the slide which was pulled by Bobby the horse to a big shed at the back of the house. It was expected to last them through the year. Jan Waye would sometimes spend a whole Sunday cutting peat. This job was also undertaken by Percy when he became older.

Another of Percy's tasks was to fetch water from the well field in two buckets attached to a hoop so that his legs did not get chafed. But, as aforementioned, a Michelmore relative suggested they look for the old well that was near the house, outside the kitchen door. It was thought it might be under a large flat rock, so some of Jan's colleagues from Redlake came over and helped lift the rock, revealing the long-hidden well, much to Percy's relief! It was cleaned out and a pump fitted in the kitchen, together with a trough. Percy Waye told the author that the water was very pure and if poured into a glass jar and held up to the light, its clarity was very apparent. Walkers given well water to drink would often comment on its quality. Given the great depth of the well, the water was extremely cold and therefore not considered suitable for livestock.

As with all Dartmoor farms, the winter's snow would cut them off for a while. But this was an eventuality for which preparations were always made. Flour would be stored in sacks and Carrie Waye would bake all her own bread and cakes. They always had a pig, a house cow for milk from which Carrie made cream and butter, and there were always eggs. The butter would be made in a wooden tub, salt added, and then made into patties.

Carrie's cooking skills were greatly appreciated by her family and Mrs Margaret Steemson, her niece, told me how she still remembers the mincepies with a little hole in the top of each one for the steam to escape. "A memory recalled each Christmas!" Carrie also made Mrs Steemson's parents' wedding cake at the warren, and it had to be carefully transported from here to Staddicombe Farm at Holne!

In the summer months, whortleberries grew in abundance on Huntingdon Hill and these would be gathered for Carrie to make into delicious pies or to serve on their own with cream. They would also be picked by the bucketful, sorted into punnets and sold. Living in such an isolated place, the Wayes made their own entertainment including folk dancing and singing. Reporting in the 1934 *Transactions of the Devonshire Association* (*TDA*), Marjory Eckett Fielden said, "Folk dancing, ie. step dancing, may still be witnessed in a few Dartmoor farm kichens, for instance, at Huntingdon Warren, Creabor and Moortown near Gidleigh, and at Coombe near Holne. ... Miss Stella Waye of Huntingdon Warren is an expert performer of the 'Broomstick' and 'Frog Dance'".[92] She also went on to say that folk songs could still be heard here too.

After Stella left school, she went into service at Hayford Hall as a general help/companion. She often accompanied her mistress to London and began a collection of postcards of Harrod's fashion department.[93] In later years, she was a dinner lady at a local school. Her husband, Mr Coles, helped in the construction of the Avon dam. Her daughter, Crystal, was born c.1936 and was the last baby to be brought up at the warren and, fittingly, was also a descendant of Thomas Michelmore, being his great-great-great-great granddaughter. Percy continued to help his father at Huntingdon Warren and, when he moved,

still retained the lands on which he continued farming.

In 1941, Huntingdon Warren was included in the National Farm Survey of England and Wales. The Survey gives a list of Jan Waye's livestock:[94]

1 cow/heifer in milk.
1 cow in calf.
30 ewes for breeding.
1 ram for service.
20 tooth ewes to be put to ram in 1941.
20 other sheep and lambs under 1 year.
12 fowls over 6 months.
10 fowls under 6 months.
1 horse.

It was during the latter part of his time at Huntingdon Warren that Jan Waye purchased an extra parcel of land at Warmacombe, near Lud Gate, on which he built a bungalow called The Stroll.[95] Initially, this was used as a winter retreat and then in 1942, when Percy married Mabel Heard, it became their home. In 1939, Jan and Carrie Waye moved to Moorside, retiring from the farming life and letting Percy take over the running of the warren.

Frederick William Symes (MooRoaMan) 1940s - 1950s

When the last of the Wayes had moved from the warren house, it was sub-let to Mr Frederick William Symes, otherwise known as 'MooRoaMan', a pseudonym under which he wrote for local newspapers. Symes, born c.1872, was the son of a Methodist minister, the Rev. Charles Symes, and during his early years, followed in his father's footsteps, travelling in a number of circuits as a lay preacher.[96] In later years, he became a schoolmaster

Carrie Waye sitting in the porch of Huntingdon Warren.

and was supposed to have been quite a classical scholar. It was upon his retirement that he went to live out at Huntingdon Warren, occupying two rooms, one up and one down. He spent the summers at this remote spot and the winters in lodgings in Buckfastleigh for which he advertised in the *Western Morning News*. He re-named the warren house 'The Lone Stead', and even had headed notepaper printed, an example of which appears in Hemery's *High Dartmoor*. One winter the house was broken into and the wooden fixtures damaged. The culprits were caught and made to repair the damage - a fitting punishment one feels!

Symes has been described as a hermit, a Dartmoor tramp, a crank and an eccentric, but was always talked of with affection. His appearance did nothing to dispel these descriptions, and perhaps Hemery provides one of the best pictures of this character when he describes "his sparkling eyes and snow-white hair emphasizing the shabbiness of his stained, rope-belted raincoat. ... He made the thickest, brownest tea of anyone I knew, brewing it in an orange-coloured tin teapot over a fire of peat and rotting timbers from the warren outhouses - and that among conditions which the prying eye advisedly ignored if his hospitality were to be stomached."[97]

Lois Deacon, in her *Dartmoor with a Difference*, also inferred that Symes was not too keen on housework, "He was reputed to do very little for himself in the house, having preferable notions for occupying his time."[98]

Dr Edward Lunt also recounted his memories of Symes. "When I first arrived at the Warren, Mr Symes was not there, but after waiting some time, I saw a strange sight of what appeared to be a moving tree on the horizon, just like Burnam Wood coming to Dunsinane in Macbeth. As it came nearer I saw that it

Frederick William Symes, also know as MooRoaMan. c.1950s.

was Mr Symes carrying a large tree branch on a yoke across his shoulders, and he stood bolt upright, so you can appreciate that he was a very fit and strong man, as he was over seventy years old at the time. He had carried it some distance on his way back from Buckfastleigh, where he walked each way most days." Dr Lunt continues, "On another occasion I took tea with Mr Symes and remember him cooking toast by placing it on the glowing surface of a peat or charcoal fire, and removing it with great skill at just the right moment to give perfect toast. We drank tea thickened with fine oatmeal, as he had no refrigerator, and told me he could not keep fresh milk during the summer months."

Symes led a solitary life at Huntingdon Warren, but he made regular trips into Buckfastleigh and Ashburton.

"At the age of 78, Frederick Symes was frequently seen walking the six miles between his home and Buckfastleigh on his way to breakfast, arriving in the stoney approach lane at six o' clock in the morning. He went to bed early in the evening and arose at dawn. Having reached Buckfastleigh, he went on, presumably by 'bus to Ashburton or Totnes for breakfast, and afterwards retramped the six miles up over to the Lonestead [sic]".[99]

Some of Symes' meals are thought to have been taken at the 'British Restaurant' in Buckfastleigh, a wartime style canteen. The author has also been told that Symes enjoyed drinking sprees in Ivybridge, returning home via the disued railway track from Cantrell to Redlake. At Michaelmas each year, he went to stay at Brimpts Farm "and enjoyed farm hospitality for a week."[100]

Postal deliveries were, by now, twice a week, and he would sometimes write letters to himself to ensure a visit from the postman.

From Huntingdon Warren, Symes continued to enjoy walking on Dartmoor and in earlier years, he had often walked the moor with Dr J.W. Malim from Torquay. In fact, Dr Malim dedicated his book *The Romance of Dartmoor* to:

Wealady, Comweal, & Mooroaman
Three staunch comrades
Who have explored the moor with me.

It was Symes who gave Huntingdon Barrow its conical-shaped top, now much reduced, and he used "gleefully to refer to its grotesqueness as appropriate to 'the Heap o' Sinners' buried beneath it."[101]

He also found "a little cavern, and this he called his chapel".[102] This may have been either the potato cave or Keble Martin's Chapel.

On 13th October 1945, Huntingdon Warren was the scene of an aircrash in which all seven crew members were killed. The American aeroplane, a Douglas C-47 Skytrain (known as a Dakota in Britain), crashed into the northern wall of the larger platt. The aeroplane was en route to Exeter but had been diverted to Plymouth due to bad weather. The *Totnes Times* carried the following report;

> "Investigations are being continued following the finding of a crashed American aircraft over the week-end on the Moor, six miles from Buckfastleigh. The 'plane, a Dakota, was heard flying over the town towards the Moor in thick fog on Saturday afternoon. Receiving a report that a machine was missing and believed to have crashed, the police organised search parties. On Sunday morning, in a pea-soup fog, the wreckage of the aircraft was found at Huntingdon Warren, in one of the loneliest spots on the Moor. The United States crew of seven were killed. All the bodies were recovered from the wreckage and taken to Ashburton whence they were sent to Cambridge for interment."[103]

Percy Waye remembers the occasion of the crash. He and his wife, Mabel, were at The Stroll and heard the aircraft overhead and thought it sounded rather low. They did not, however, hear the crash. The next day, Percy accompanied the police out to the wreckage and found that some of it had been scattered as far as the

Frederick William Symes, taken towards the end of his life.

Heap o' Sinners. He noticed in some of the metalwork bullet holes from World War Two.

Whether Symes was at Huntingdon Warren when the crash occurred is not known; probably not or he would have reported it the same day to the Wayes. But he did collect a few souvenirs from the wreckage. "The inside of his house, indescribably derelict, was decorated with the propellor and other trophies from an aircraft which had crashed outside."[104]

At the age of 84, Symes decided life at Huntingdon Warren was no longer feasible. The isolation and the long trips into town for provisions must have become rather tedious. So he moved to Buckfastleigh on a permanent basis, and then in early 1961, he moved to Kingsteignton. Later that year, he died, at the age of 89 at Newton Abbot Hospital. His funeral took place at the Courtenay Street Methodist Church in Newton Abbot, and he was buried at Albaston, near Gunnislake in Cornwall.[105]

Meanwhile, shortly after Symes had left the warren for the last time in 1956, the house was burnt down. In the August, a group of campers, reputed to have been naval cadets, failed to extinguish a fire they had lit in an upstairs room and it took a hold on the house, the occupants only just managing to escape without injury to themselves. So for the second time in its history, the house was gutted by fire, only this time it was never to be rebuilt. In July 1961, the Duchy decided the ruins were "dangerous to man and beast" and called in contractors to pull them down.[106] A lone

Huntingdon Warren 1955.

sycamore tree now marks the site. In 1984, the Dartmoor National Park Committee rejected a Duchy of Cornwall proposal to rebuild the house and install a shepherd in it.[107]

Percy Waye relinquished his lease on Huntingdon Warren in the late 1970s, and thus ended the Michelmore association which had endured for at least 175 years, with only one short break.

REFERENCES

1. Court Rolls, Dartmoor 1479. PRO 166/48. With thanks to Dr Tom Greeves for help in relocating this reference
2. Robertson, J. "The Archaeology of the Upper Plym Valley". Ph.D thesis University of Edinburgh 1991 pp.254-5
3. Haynes, R.G. Unpublished MS c.1969 Plymouth City Library
4. loc. cit.
5. Crossing, W. *Crossing's Guide to Dartmoor* David & Charles 1976 p.366
6. Crossing, W. *Crossing's Dartmoor Worker* David & Charles 1966 p.60
7. Gill, C.(Ed.) *The Duchy of Cornwall* David & Charles 1987 p.46
8. "Memorials of the Family Trist" n.d. Totnes Museum
9. DCO(L) Lease dated 1809
10. DRO(Exeter) 47/9/2/15 Trist Settlement Document 1799 and *Trewman's Exeter Flying Post* 28.5.1801
11. "Memorials of the Family Trist"
12. loc. cit.
13. DRO(Exeter) op. cit.
14. DRO(Exeter) Z17/3/8 Simpson, W. "Survey of the Forest of Dartmoor Belonging to HRH the Prince of Wales" 1786
15. *Trewman's Exeter Flying Post* op. cit.
16. Caton, M. Letter to author: 7.12.1992
17. Crossing, W. "Crockern Tor & the Ancient Stannary Parliament" in *The Western Antiquary* Vol 9 p.5
18. Crossing, W. *Crossing's Dartmoor Worker* p.60
19. Waye, P. Oral info. given to author: 4.1.1990
20. Parish Registers, Buckfastleigh
21. DCO(L) Box 57. Huntingdon Warren docket. Letter: 1.3.1802
22. ibid. Letter:7.7.1806
23. loc. cit.
24. DCO(L) Lease Plan, 1809
25. Crossing, W. "Crockern Tor & its Ancient Stannary Parliament" p.6
26. Waye, P. op. cit.
27. DCO(L) Box 57. Letter: 1866
28. Worth, R.H. *Worth's Dartmoor* David & Charles 1981 p.417
29. Crossing, W. *Amid Devonia's Alps* David & Charles 1974 p.35
30. Waye, P. op. cit.
31. loc. cit.
32. Crossing, W. *Dartmoor's Early Historic & Medieval Remains* Quay Publications (Brixham) 1987
33. ibid. p.40
34. DCO(L) Box 17. Huntingdon Warren docket. 1890
35. Waye, P. op. cit.
36. DCO(L) op. cit. "Epitome of the Title of Mr William Michelmore to the Leasehold Property Known as Huntingdon Warren Lidford". June 1882
37. Thomas Michelmore's Will, 1840
38. DCO(L) op. cit.
39. DCO(B) Huntingdon Warren docket. Letter: 2.8.1852
40. DCO(L) op. cit. Letter: 1852
41. loc. cit.
42. Greeves, T. Notes on Huntingdon Mine.
43. loc. cit.
44. Hemery, E. *High Dartmoor* Robert Hale Ltd 1983 p.311
45. DCO(L) op. cit. Letter: 25.11.1861
46. ibid. Letter: 8.11.1882
47. ibid. Letter 1882
48. Greeves, T. op. cit.
49. Crossing, W. *Amid Devonia's Alps* p.41
50. Greeves, T. op. cit.
51. loc. cit.

52. Waye, P. Oral info. given to author: 27.5.1992
53. DCO(L) op. cit. Letter: 10.12.1880
54. *British Hunts & Huntsmen* The Biographical Press 1908 p.483
55. DCO(L) op. cit. Letter: 4.12.1882
56. O'Hara, J. Oral info. given to author 1990 and Tozer, E. *The South Devon Hunt* Privately Published 1916 p.174
57. DCO(L) op. cit. Letter: 6.3.1881
58. ibid. Letter: 24.3.1881
59. DCO(L) Box 11. Huntingdon Warren docket. Letter: Sept 1882
60. DCO(L) Box 17. Letter: 3.11.1882
61. ibid. Letter: 29.11.1882
62. ibid. Letter: 7.4.1886
63. Crossing, W. *Crossing's Dartmoor Worker* p.60
64. DRO(Exeter) Coombe School Attendance Book
65. Electoral Registers, Lydford
66. DCO(L) op. cit. Letter: 21.2.1890
67. loc. cit.
68. ibid. Letter: 16.2.1890
69. ibid. Letter: 24.9.1890
70. Census Returns, Lydford and Electoral Registers, Lydford
71. Harbord, A. "Young Keble Martin on Dartmoor" in *The Countryman* Autumn 1973 p.47
72. Harbord, A. Oral info. given to author 1990
73. Harbord, A. "Young Keble Martin on Dartmoor" p.46
74. Wade, E. *The Redlake Tramway* Twelveheads Press 1982 p.20
75. loc. cit.
76. China Clay Company File. PRO BT31/19202/107532
77. DRO(Exeter) Coombe School Attendance Book.
78. PRO IR58/66261
79. Steemson, Mrs M. Letter to author: 23.1.1992
80. Electoral Registers, Lydford
81. loc. cit.
82. Ivybridge & District Amenity Society Newsletter Winter 1985
83. *Totnes Times* 23.10.1920
84. ibid. 12.11.27
85. DRO(Exeter) Coombe, Holne and Ugborough School Attendance Books
86. Fielden, M.E. "Humerous Happenings in Devon" in *The Devonian Yearbook* 1937
87. Ivybridge & District Amenity Society Newsletter op. cit.
88. loc. cit.
89. loc. cit.
90. Fox, H. "There's Rosemary and Rue" Unpublished MS 1974
91. loc. cit.
92. Fielden, M.E. "Old Time Survivals in Devon" in *TDA* Vol 66
93. Stone, N. Oral info. given to author: 1989
94. PRO MAF32/679/351
95. The Scorriton & District Review c.1980s
96. *Western Morning News* 28.4.61
97. Hemery, E, op. cit. p.312
98. Deacon, L. *Dartmoor With a Difference* Toucan Press 1973 p.27
99. loc. cit.
100. ibid. p.22
101. Hemery, E. op. cit. p.312
102. Deacon, L. op. cit. p.27
103. *Totnes Times* 20.10.1945
104. Deacon, L. op. cit.
105. *Western Morning News*
106. Cronin, R. Oral info. given to author: 1993. Based on information obtained from the Duchy of Cornwall.
107. DNP Committee Minute 845, 1984

7. WHITESLADE OR SNAILY HOUSE

Situated on the left bank of the East Dart river, on the western slopes of Riddon Ridge, at SX 611 764, is the ruin of Whiteslade House, otherwise known as 'Snaily House'. It stands at a height of 985 ft (300m) above sea level. From what remains of the house, which is very little, the fireplace, cupboard recesses and window spaces are still visible, as are the attached barns and outbuildings, all of which would have been thatched. There may have been a pot-water leat taken off the East Dart, but the planting of conifers in the area during the 1930s has made field evidence inconclusive. To the north of the house are four upright granite stones which may have had use as a stackstand or staddles. In the river below the house are Snaily Steps giving access to the other side of the East Dart.

The tale of 'Snaily House' has become firmly imbedded in Dartmoor's folklore. Two elderly spinster sisters lived at the house. They always looked well nourished, yet were never seen purchasing groceries from neighbouring villages or farms. Suspicion and curiosity were aroused in the minds of the local people, who took it upon themselves to investigate. Paying the two ladies an unwelcome visit, they searched the premises of Snaily House for evidence of stolen vegetables and livestock. They found nothing. However, a large lidded pan caught the eye of one individual who, upon lifting the lid, saw a great quantity of salted-down black slugs, which he then showed to the other 'visitors'. The two old ladies were so humiliated that the nature of their diet had been exposed, they pined away and eventually died. Upon their deaths, Snaily House, as it was from thereon known, began crumbling into the ruin we see today. Baring-Gould wrote his own version of this tale in his *Dartmoor Idylls*.

It has to be said that this folktale exists in other parts of the country and in the Channel Islands. The name 'Snaily House' is also attached to other Dartmoor areas. The abundance of black slugs, often called snails in country areas were, no doubt, used to supplement diets, but it seems probable that the story of the two spinster sisters at Whiteslade has no foundation.

Documentary evidence to support the story has not been forthcoming. The only reference to snails at Whiteslade is in a Forestry Commission booklet by G.D. Rouse[1] who claims that French Napoleonic prisoners of war built the house and imported snails from France to eat! On discussing the matter with him, Mr Rouse said he had relied upon oral information which he felt to be dubious. D. Brunsden, in another book,[2] takes up the theme of Napoleonic prisoners of war working on the newtake, but he cannot recall the source of his claim. However, Rouse's booklet appears in his bibliography, which is probably where the answer

The interior of Whiteslade showing the rubble-filled fireplace and the cupboards to the right.

lies. The records relating to the Napoleonic prisoners of war, held in the Public Record Office, do not mention Whiteslade.

Tracing the origins of the Whiteslade enclosure proved challenging. The original newtake seems to have been taken from the moor in the 1700s by Thomas Hamlyn of Brimpts, who also had Winford on the opposite side of the East Dart.[3] Whiteslade would have been an appropriate name for a Brimpts newtake as 'white' was a term often applied to an outer piece of property or land. It can also mean wide. 'Slade' means land 'lying low and moist'.

Whiteslade in 1902.

It is unlikely that the newtake existed before 1702. The well documented lawsuit of Thomas Bernaford, the rector of Lydford in that year, other than listing the ancient tenements, mentions the other existing 'divers newtakes'. Winford is one of these, belonging to Thomas Hamlyn Jr., but Whiteslade is not listed, indicating that it had not yet been built. Hemery

maintains Whiteslade House is ancient, but there is no evidence to support this and, in fact, the original newtake did not extend as far north as the dwelling, being only the customary eight acres.

That the newtake was originally much smaller is shown in the Lydford Court Roll of 8th July 1721. Thomas Hamlyn surrendered to Richard Wills the copyhold inheritance of "one close of land containing eight acres of land or thereabouts known by the name of or commonly called Whiteslade ... in Riddon Ridge, abutting on Winford".[4] There are no references to Whiteslade in the Court Rolls before 1721, so it is possible Hamlyn acquired the newtake in this year.

Richard Wills held the land for 16 years, at a rent of 1s per acre, and then, in 1737, he surrendered it to Richard Brooking.[5] Upon Brooking's death in 1775, his son Richard took it over together with Winford.[6] Brooking junior sub-let Whiteslade, still only eight acres in size, to John French and later, to George Veal.[7]

By now, as in prehistoric and medieval times, Riddon Ridge was being divided into parcels of land,[8] all of which were unwalled except that of Whiteslade. This suggests the Whiteslade enclosure was used for crops and that walls were necessary to keep out the livestock grazing on the open moor. Boundary stones were used to divide the rest of the ridge and a few remain today although not all in situ. The 'TS' and 'TS/H' stones belonged to Thomas Smerdon, erected c.1754. The 'RHR' stones belonged to Robert Henley Rogers Esq., while the 'SL' stone to be found leaning up against the Whiteslade barn belonged to the Rev. Samuel Lane of Totnes who leased a Babeny tenement.[9] It is not know when the 'RHR' and 'SL' stones were erected. Rev. Lane had the Babeny tenement certainly by 1810[10] and upon his death his son, another Samuel, took over the lease in 1834. Robert Henley Roger's father was Sir Frederick

The barn at Whiteslade or 'Snaily House'
after the forest clearance, 1992. Note the
'SL' stone propped up against the end right wall.

Leman Rogers of Blatchford in Cornwood who, in 1754, acquired the lease on two of the Babeny tenements and Babeny Rutt[sic].[11] He died in 1797 and in his will the Babeny tenements were left to his third son, Robert Henley, who was a minor at the time of his father's death.[12] As a naval captain, Robert Henley was often away at sea, so it is possible that his brother, Sir John, handled the estate for him. Sir John is referred to in *Dartmoor - A New Study* in connection with Babeny in 1810.

At some time between Sir Frederick's death and the sale of Babeny by the Rogers family in 1813,[13] Robert Henley acquired the land on Riddon Ridge defining the area with his initialled boundstones. It has been suggested in several books that these stones were the bounds of tinners, but there is no evidence to support this claim. Rev. Lane and Robert Henley Rogers were associated with Babeny farms. The name Smerdon is also associated with farming; branches of this family lived in the parishes of Lydford and Widecombe including the hamlet of Cator nearby. No documentary source has yet been found to suggest the stones and their owners had tinworking connections. There is also little field evidence of tinworking in the immediate area other than what appear to be trial pits on the ridge.

There is another interesting stone on Riddon Ridge which has an incised cross on it, between Riddon Farm and Bellever, just below the large hut circle. It may have been on a route connecting the ancient tenement of Riddon with the old Lych Way. Riddon Farm is first documented in 1488 but it is likely to have existed as an ancient tenement long before then.

In 1784, while George Veal was still farming Whiteslade, Brooking surrendered it, together with Winford, to Rev. William Moore[14] and, as a consequence, it also became known as 'Moore's Newtake'. Still only eight acres in size, no house had yet been built, but Moore was to change this. Veal continued as sub-tenant until 1794.[15] Then for four years the tenancy was vacant. It is likely to have been during this period that the newtake was extended to its present size, and the house erected; they had certainly been completed by 1802.[16]

Samuel Wills had become the sub-tenant of Whiteslade by 1798, and he remained as such until 1816.[17] As his is the only name other than Moore's to be associated with the newtake in the Land Tax Assessment lists, it can be assumed he lived in the house until c.1812. Moore himself was living in Chagford. From 1797 to 1810, he lived in Rushford Cottage with a Mr George Pike. In 1810, he became Rector of Chagford Church until his death in 1819. For some of this time, he lived in the Glebe with a Mr Hewings.[18]

By 1813, Wills had sub-let Whiteslade to farm labourer, William Stook,[19] and had either moved out or

Hazel Stook Pattison (right) standing in the ruins of Whiteslade on 29th March 1990. This was once the home of her great-great-grandfather, William Stook and her great grandfather, Richard Stook, in the early 1800s.

Trough in Snaily House plantation.

lived under the same roof. William and his wife, Mary (née French from Babeny), had four sons, John, William, Richard and George. In March 1990, the author was fortunate enough to meet the great-great-granddaughter of William and Mary Stook, Mrs Hazel Stook Pattison, who resided in the USA. Sadly, she has since died, but not before she was able to visit her ancestors' home. She also paid a visit to Babeny, home of Mary before her marriage to William in 1804, where she was shown the ruins of the ancient longhouse by the farmer, Mr Wilkinson.

Rev. Moore sold Whiteslade to the Rev. John White in 1816 for the sum of £200.[20] Rev. White acquired Dury and 'Lafter Heath' in that year too. In 1813, he had bought Babeny from the Rogers family for the sum of £1950.[21] He also leased Bellever and two Merripits.[22]

Not wanting to live at Whiteslade himself, Rev. White let it to William Pooke, another farm labourer, and his family. In 1821, Pooke's wife, Elizabeth, gave birth to their son, John. Three years later, their daughter, Elizabeth, was baptised.[23] At some stage, Rev. White lived at Merryfield Farm at Woodland near Ashburton and sub-let the Babeny tenement and lands to John and Thomas Irish. That Rev. White still owned Whiteslade is evidenced by the Tithe Map. This also shows the slated barn to the east of the house had not yet been erected; this was done a few years later at a cost of £35.[24]

The Tithe Map also tells us that the newtake had been divided into several fields, many of them described as 'brake' or 'waste' land. Two of the thirteen fields were listed as arable, suggesting that livestock was kept. A garden was situated by the house, and a road went from the house roughly south through the newtake down to the East Dart at the northern wall of the original newtake. Gates in the walls of the older newtake gave access to Winford and Babeny. Today, to the north east of the barn can be seen an enclosed field with high walls not dissimilar to the platts at Huntingdon Warren. In the wall just below the barn is what looks like a partially collapsed kennel or similar structure. In another field is a possible clearance cairn.

By 1841, detailed census returns had appeared, and those for that year show Whiteslade was occupied by Edward Caunter and Elizabeth Kivill, both in their 60s and listed as agricultural labourers. It is possible that Edward and Elizabeth were related. Elizabeth was born in 1776, the illegitimate daughter of Elizabeth Stidson, and her middle name was Caunter, suggesting her father was from this family.[25] She married Abraham Kivill and they lived at Jordan Mill near Widecombe. Widowed in 1820, she no doubt had to work for an income, thus explaining why she is living at Whiteslade in 1841. After leaving Whiteslade sometime before 1848, she returned to the Jordan area - Drywells farm - where she died in 1858.[26]

It is in the 1841 census returns that the first known reference to the house being called 'Snails House' occurs. Salting down of black slugs, commonly found on Dartmoor, was practised amongst country folk to supplement their diet or to sell at market. In Eden Phillpott's *The American Prisoner*, Lovey Lee sold salted-down slugs at the Princetown market. Although a fictitious character, this would not have been unlikely. So Edward and Elizabeth may well have used slugs to supplement their diet and income. The name has stayed with the house thanks to authors such as Baring-Gould and Crossing.

In 1848, Whiteslade was being tenanted by the Frenches, and in that year, Susannah French died aged 34.[27] From 1850 to 1851, Thomas and Martha Isaac tenanted the house and newtake, with their children, Sarah and Jonas Coaker. Betsy Stancombe died at Whiteslade in 1852 and was either lodging with the Isaacs or was, herself, a tenant, replacing them.[28]

Billing's Directory for 1857 shows farmer William Widdicombe living there, but by 1861 he too had moved on. Early in 1861, Rev. White let Richard Mann of Dunstone Farm and Mr Mason of Great Dunstone, Widecombe, become tenants, and they sub-let it to Elizabeth Coaker, a widow with four children, William, George, Albert and Elizabeth. They also had a lodger, agricultural labourer John Mathews.[29]

The house, by this time, was in a very bad state of repair which may have been a contributory factor to the Coakers moving out later in 1861. In January 1862, Rev. White's sons, Matthew and John, became the owners of Whiteslade, their father having died. They also held the estates of Dury and Lafter Heath newtake. These properties were freehold, meaning that at some time they had passed out of Duchy control, but details have not been found. Matthew decided to try and sell all three estates to the Duchy of Cornwall for the sum of £1100.[30] However, they discovered he was not in a position to sell as his brother was joint owner. John's permission must have been obtained because negotiations re-started. Matthew decided to ask £320 for Whiteslade and invited the Duchy to inspect the property.[31] Taking up this invitation, they consequently disagreed as to the sum asked, and suggested £175 was more reasonable. This went down none too well with Matthew and, as Barrington said, "he is quite determined not to sell it for less than £200 being the amount I understand his father gave for it."[32]

Taking into consideration the barn erected at the expense of £35, the Duchy finally agreed to pay the £200, on condition that he also sold Dury and Lafter Heath too. This condition was met.

It is in Barrington's letter, part of which was quoted above, that we learn of the condition of the house, and it is apparent that with the Coakers, it had sheltered its last inhabitants. "The dwelling house is in a very dilapidated state and which in the event of acquiring

Two views of Whiteslade in 1912.

During 1991 and 1992, the trees were felled and, at the time of writing, the Forestry Commission are considering disposal of the land as part of their rationalisation programme and to aid the improvement of the landscape on Dartmoor. Preliminary discussions are under way with the Duchy of Cornwall.[35] Downstream from Snaily House, on the left bank of the East Dart, are some steps leading down to the river's edge. They do not appear to be that old and may have some connection with the Forestry Commission, although they had no record of their construction. It has also been suggested they were to give access to the river's edge for fishermen.

So the social history of Whiteslade or Snaily House came to a close in the 1860s but not as a result of two elderly spinster sisters dying of humiliation. That slugs were collected, salted-down and sold, and even eaten at the farm is plausible, but the romanticised tale is nothing more than that.

the tenement, I do not think it would be desirable to restore."[33]

Another document written at this time confirms that the house was 'dilapidated' and unoccupied.[34]

The land continued to be used for summering cattle by local farmers until it was sold to the Forestry Commission and planted with conifers in 1935. This made access to the ruins of Whiteslade difficult.

REFERENCES

1. Rouse, G.D. *The New Forests of Dartmoor* HMSO 1964 p.12
2. Brunsden, D. *Dartmoor* The Geographical Society 1968 p.39
3. Moore, S. & Birkett, P. *A Short History of the Rights of Common Upon the Forest of Dartmoor and the Commons of Devon* DPA 1890 p.90
4. DCO(L) Box S/2. Court Roll, Lydford 8.7.1721
5. ibid. 5.12.1737
6. ibid. 16.10.1775
7. LTA's, Lydford
8. DCO(L) Miscellaneous Papers 1814
9. loc. cit.
10. loc. cit.

11. Hankin, Charles. Information given to author based on documents in the WDRO.
12. loc. cit.
13. loc. cit.
14. DCO(L) Court Rolls, Lydford 15.5.1784
15. LTA's, Lydford
16. West Country Studies Library (Exeter) O.S. Surveyors Drawings 1802-3
17. LTA's, Lydford
18. LTA's, Chagford
19. Parish Registers, Widecombe
20. DCO(L) Box 11. Whiteslade docket. Letter: 14.2.1862
21. Hankin, Charles op. cit.
22. LTA's, Lydford
23. Parish Registers, Widecombe
24. DCO(L) op. cit. Letter: 14.2.1862
25. Parish Registers, Widecombe
26. loc. cit.
27. loc. cit.
28. loc. cit.
29. Census Returns, Lydford
30. DCO(L) op. cit. Letter: 1862
31. ibid. Letter: 23.1.1862
32. ibid. Letter: 14.2.1862
33. loc. cit.
34. DCO(L) Box 6. Whiteslade docket. Letter: 2.7.1880
35. Hunt, J. Forest District Manager. Letter to author: 21.1.1993

8. BROWN'S HOUSE

The ruin of Brown's House, situated about half a mile north west of Lower White Tor, at SX 615 798, and 1590 feet (485m) above sea level, has often intrigued people, partly because of its remoteness and unaccommodating terrain and partly because Dartmoor literature has yielded so little information.

Attached to the ruin is some folklore not dissimilar to that of the two Dolly Trebble Cotts near Brimpts and at Swincombe. Brown, described by Baring-Gould as an ungainly man, morose in character, built the house in which to confine his pretty young wife and keep her safe from the attentions of other admirers.[1]

Brown's House is rightly attributed to a man named Brown. His full name was Dr Benjamin Hayward Brown and he was a "Doctor in Physic"[2] who came from Withecombe near Chagford. In 1810, encouraged by the successful attempts of 'improvers' to enclose large tracts of moorland with the intention of establishing farms, Brown decided to try his luck too, but without waiting for the Duchy of Cornwall's agreement to grant him a lease.

Dr Brown had, in fact, applied for a 99 year lease in May 1810, but due to the wheels of bureaucracy moving slowly, several months elapsed during which he became impatient and commenced work on his chosen plot of 305 acres.[3] The bounds for which he applied abutted "North upon Mether Hill, East upon Cherrybrook and Hollocombe Hill, South East and South upon the Inclosure of the Revd James Holman Mason, and South West and West upon Crouter Hill".[4] Rev. Mason had enclosed several hundreds of acres extending north from the area around Crockern Tor. Crouter Hill refers to the Crow and Row/Rough Tor area and Mether Hill is now known as Wildbanks Hill, on which the northern boundary wall was built.

Upon this land, Brown had applied to build "one good and substantial messuage or Farm House with suitable outbuildings".[5]

The Duchy were not amused when they discovered Brown had not waited to secure a lease, and when it was finally granted in January 1811, Brown, in turn, was not amused to discover the level of rent he was expected to pay; 1s. 6d. per acre an annum, whereas other lessees were paying 1s per acre.[6] Brown had already incurred considerable expense and employment of labour in developing the land, so he found himself in a dilemma. To proceed with establishing the farm would cause financial difficulties for himself and his dependants, but to abandon the fruits of his labours would be to lose the money he had already invested in the project.

The Duchy were not sympathetic. Their reason for imposing such a high rent reflected their increasing concern with the escalating rate at which moorland was being enclosed, saying they wished to "check the avidity with which grants of this kind were so generally sought after."[7] However, they did reduce the rent per acre to 1s. 3d. or £19. 2s. per annum. This

The ruins of Brown's House showing one of the gateposts to the left.

was because Brown, at his own expense, was expected to build a road to the farm, which would have been very expensive, but which would undoubtedly increase the value of the farm.[8]

Access to this remote spot would have been from Postbridge, via Drift Lane, Braddons Lake Ford, up to Rowter Gate, north of Rowter Rocks, across the upper reaches of the Cherrybrook and westwards to the house (Crossing uses both spellings of 'Rowter' and 'Rowtor'). This last section was described by Crossing as "really a good hard road".[9] It continues to the West Dart and westwards over the Cowsic river and Conies

The gateposts leading to Brown's House and garden.

Brown's House. The fireplace lintel can be seen in the centre.

Down where, according to Crossing, it joins up with the Lych Way track. The track from Drift Lane to Brown's House is still used today by walkers, and thus it remains well defined in parts.

The house itself was erected fairly quickly. Having read the edition of *Risdon's Survey of Devon* published in 1811, it seems his editors mistakenly included Brown's land in with that of Mr Paterson's, whose 3000 acres had been taken over by brothers Thomas and John Hullett for establishing the settlement of Postbridge. The editors comment that there is "a considerable quantity of ground banked in by Mr Paterson, on which, however, besides the erection of a house, but little appears to have been done."[10]

This may well have been Brown's House as it fits its description of a single house with surrounding banks forming some of the boundary walls. Hemery also believed this to be the case, although he seemed unaware of Mr Paterson's interests in the Postbridge area, suggesting that he was Brown's 'man'! The editors instead link Dr Brown with land "on the verge of the Forest near Oakhampton [sic]"[11] which is inaccurate. Whether or not the house mentioned was Dr Brown's, it was certainly finished by 1812, together with the outbuilding.[12]

Today, there is little to show for Dr Brown's labours. Two gateposts leaning in on each other mark the entrance to the home field where perhaps potatoes were once grown. Having passed through the gateposts, the ruins of what was almost certainly a single storey dwelling, are on the right where the doorway in the eastern wall is still evident. Going through the doorway, one is in the main room, with a smaller one off to the left. The larger room measures 18' 6" x 16' (5.6m x 4.9m) approximately, while the smaller one is about 18' 6" x 8' 8" (5.6m x 2.7m) A fireplace was built in the western wall of the larger room and the lintel and uprights can still be seen lying in the rubble of what is left of the walls.

The water supply may have come from a spring in the home field but the area is now badly overgrown by the vegetation so it is not easy to say for sure. Hemery claims a pot-water leat was taken off the upper Cherrybrook to the farm for another water supply. No trace of this leat has yet been found on the ground, but an aerial photograph[13] shows a leat coming from the West Dart, a branch of which passes the farmhouse. This leat may pre-date Brown's House as it appears that an original course leads to tin workings to the south.

To the south of the house lies a small building with internal measurements of 15' x 6' 6" (4.57m x 1.98m). Although having been described elsewhere as a shippen,[14] this was in fact a tinners' building[15] and is situated amongst the workings. Brown may have made use of it too, but it does pre-date the farm.

It is cattle that would have been farmed out here. According to oral information received from John Hamlyn in 1981, who was then aged 98, he had heard that butter and milk had been produced at Brown's House during the Napoleonic Wars and sold to the French prisoners of war.[16]

The boundary walls were never finished, and one need only glance at the O.S. Outdoor Leisure Map to see this. Crossing felt that had the farm survived it would have been named 'Rowter Farm' and comments that it was due to Brown's House that the area became known as Rowter; "The name of the tor became attached to this area in consequence of the latter forming what was probably to have been Rowter Farm".[17]

In June 1812, having constructed the buildings and some of the boundary walls, Brown, for reasons undisclosed, sold the lease for £700 to Mr Matthew

The tinners' hut among the old mining workings near Brown's House.

Walbank, a gentleman from Bubble Well, Minchinhampton in Gloucestershire.[18] The rent was substantially reduced to £7. 12s. 3d. per annum because the proposed road had not been built. In the event of its construction, the rent would be increased. The name Walbank in connection with Brown's House and enclosures is interesting. Crossing and subsequent writers refer to part of the enclosure walls as Wildbanks Newtake. It seems likely that this is a corruption of Walbank. Mether Hill in the lease, upon which Brown had his northern boundary, is today known as Wildbanks Hill.

Once in possession of Dr Brown's house and newtake, Walbank promptly mortgaged the property to secure a loan of £1000 with interest.[19] The gentleman from whom he obtained his mortgage was his cousin and half brother-in-law, Rev. Robert Lawrence Townsend, who lived at Steanbridge, Painswick in Gloucestershire. This mortgage was paid off by 1815.

In 1818, proposals for a railroad across Dartmoor were being mooted by Sir Thomas Tyrwhitt, founder of Princetown, and he submitted his scheme to the Chamber of Commerce in Plymouth. Briefly, the line was to run from Princetown to Crabtree near Plymouth for the purpose of transporting resources plundered from Dartmoor's terrain, and commodities to be brought onto the moor for its cultivation, such as lime, coal and timber. This has been well documented elsewhere, but the possibility of this railroad meant that the Duchy saw an opportunity to raise Walbank's rent on its completion,[20] due no doubt to their feeling this newtake would be less remote and therefore of more value.

They may also have favoured increasing the rent due to a not so well known fact that c. 1818, a road was proposed from Crockern Tor Farm to Okehampton, running east of Longaford Tor and west of the White Tors, near Brown's House, and on northwards across the moor.[21] Had it been built, it would have been of considerable convenience to Walbank. It could be that part of the route was already an alternative trackway to his house.

By 1818, Walbank had moved to Moretonhampstead.[22] His residence in this town meant that he must have sub-let the farm to a tenant. It was in this year that he entered into an agreement with Mr Robert Strong of Chilcombe near Bridport in Dorset and Mr George Whitehead, his trustee.[23] Strong agreed to purchase an annuity of £40 for three lives, being his own and those of the Rev. Henry Strangeways, Rector of Moreton in Dorset, and the Rev. Houlton Hartwell Clerk, Vicar of Loders, also in Dorset. Should Walbank fail to pay the £40, Strong and Whitehead had the power to enter his premises after 20 days and distrain and impound what goods they felt necessary for the recovery of the amount due.[24]

In August 1820, an agreement of a similar nature was drawn up between Walbank and Mr William Henry Douce of Bath and Mr Henry Mant of Bath, his trustee.[25] Again, the annuity purchased for the sum of £400, was for £40. The three lives were for those of William Douce and his son and daughter, Henry and Margaret Catherine. The same terms applied regarding any failure of Walbank's part to pay the annuity.[26]

At some stage Walbank, who was experiencing financial difficulties, sub-let the farm to George Gillard of Upton Hellions, near Crediton. Writing to the Duchy in June 1829, a concerned Mr Gillard wrote that although he still had the property, "from the presumption that there still is a considerable arrear of High Rent due — as also of interest on a mortgage created by him, I have been afraid to stock or make any profit or advantage of the property which therefore, remains in a very dilapidated state.

Mr Walbank from his embarrased [sic] situation never completed his contract or assigned the property to me, nor do I think there is any chance of my compelling him to do so — or reimbursing myself the heavy losses I have sustained on his account. Mr Mason has therefore suggested that under breach of covenant by non-payment of the High Rent the lease is forfeited and the Dutchy [sic] has a right to re-enter.

I am therefore induced to ask whether (to enable me to put the house and premises in repair) you will permit me to become tennant for a fresh term or for the residue of the present one — on payment of the present High Rent (regularly) which I believe is £7. 10s. per ann."[27]

The outcome of this matter has not been found.

It is in 1829 that references to Brown's House ceased in the records. It is likely it was abandoned soon afterwards, the remoteness and inaccessibility of the property not being conducive to living there. Certainly, there are no references to it in the parish registers, the Tithe Map and early census returns. We know, from visiting the site, that Walbank never finished building the enclosure walls Brown started. Baring-Gould, writing in 1900 records that elderly locals to whom he spoke could "remember when the chimney fell",[28] which would have been some time after it had been abandoned.

The establishment of a farm in this particular location must have been an uphill struggle. Transportation of materials to the plot, not found in situ, would have been difficult and expensive. Persuading a potential sub-tenant not only to farm the land but to live in the lonely house itself would not have been easy. Who would want to endure endless days of mist, relentless rain and Dartmoor winters out here, with lack of easy access to the nearest settlement and with no other human habitation in sight? To quote Baring-Gould again, "it is in so remote a spot that only the shepherd, the rush-cutter and the occasional fisherman approach it."[29]

That the road was never built by Walbank, and that the farm was abandoned after only a few years suggests, amongst other problems, financial difficulties. Perhaps Brown's House is an apt example of the old Dartmoor saying, "If you scratch my back, I'll tear out your pocket".

REFERENCES

1. Baring-Gould, S. *A Book of Dartmoor* Methuen & Co London 1900 p165
2. DCO(L) Lease Book 1811 - 1818
3. loc. cit.
4. loc. cit.
5. loc. cit.
6. loc. cit.
7. loc. cit.
8. Crossing, W. *Crossing's Guide to Dartmoor* David & Charles 1976 p.118
9. ibid. p.54
10. Risdon, Tristram, *The Chorographical Description or Survey of the County of Devon* Rees & Curtis, Plymouth 1714 (1811 edition with editor's notes) p.410
11. loc. cit.
12. DCO(L) Lease Book 1818 - 1825
13. RCHME Ref. 106G/UK/894
14. Hemery, E. *High Dartmoor* Robert Hale Ltd 1983 p.423
15. Greeves, T. Oral info. given to author: 13.12.1992
16. Oral information given to T. Greeves on 4th February 1981.
17. Crossing, W. op. cit. p.117
18. DCO(L) op. cit.
19. DCO(L) Lease Book 1818-1825
20. DCO(L) Lease Book 1811-1818
21. DCO(L) Lease Plans 1818
22. DCO(L) Lease Book 1818-1825
23. loc. cit.
24. loc. cit.
25. loc. cit.
26. loc. cit.
27. DCO (L) Dartmoor Box 60
28. Baring-Gould, S. op. cit. p.164
29. loc. cit.

BIBLIOGRAPHY

Baring-Gould, Sabine, *A Book of Dartmoor* Methuen 1900

Baring-Gould, Sabine, *Devonshire Characters and Strange Events* The Bodley Head Ltd 1926

Billings, M., *Directory and Gazetteer of the County of Devon* 1857

British Hunts and Huntsmen The Biographical Press 1908

Brunsden, Denys *Dartmoor* The Geographical Association 1968

Burnard, R. *Dartmoor Pictorial Records* Devon Books (facsimile reprint of 1890-1894 vols) 1986

Carrington, N.T. *Dartmoor: A Descriptive Poem* John Murray 1826

Cocks, J.V. Somers 'The Boundary of the Forest of Dartmoor on the North-Eastern Side' *DCNQ* 30 1967

Crossing, William, *Amid Devonia's Alps* David & Charles 1974

Crossing, W. *The Ancient Crosses of Dartmoor, with a Description of Their Surroundings* C.E. Mathews & J.G. Commin 1887

Crossing, W. *The Ancient Stone Crosses of Dartmoor and its Borderland* J.G. Commin 1902

Crossing, W. 'Crockern Tor and the Ancient Stannary Parliament' *Western Antiquity* Vols 8,9,10,11; 1889,1890,1891

Crossing, W. *Crossing's Dartmoor Worker* David & Charles 1966

Crossing, W. *Dartmoor's Early Historic & Medieval Remains* Quay Publications (Brixham) 1987

Crossing, W. *Guide to Dartmoor* Western Morning News 1909

Crossing, W. *One Hundred Years on Dartmoor* Western Morning News, 1901

Crossing, W. *Princetown - Its Rise and Progress* Quay Publications (Brixham) 1989

Crossing, W. *The Teign from Moor to Sea* Quay Publications (Brixham) 1986

Day, K. *Eden Phillpotts on Dartmoor* David & Charles 1981

Deacon, L. *Dartmoor with a Difference* Toucan Press 1973

Devon & Cornwall Notes & Queries, various

Devon Historian, The, various

Fielden, M. Eckett 'Old-time Survivals in Devon' *TDA* 1934

Fox, H. There's Rosemary and Rue Unpublished MS 1974

Gill, C. (Ed.) *Dartmoor: A New Study* David & Charles 1970

Gill, C. (Ed.) *The Duchy of Cornwall* David & Charles 1987

Greaves, R. *A Short History of the Dartmoor Hunt* Reid-Hamilton c.1950

Greeves, T. *Tin Mines and Miners of Dartmoor* Devon Books 1986

Gregg, P. *A Social and Economic History of Britain 1760-1972* George G. Harrap & Co Ltd 1977

Harbord, A. 'Young Keble Martin on Dartmoor' *The Countryman* Autumn 1973

Harris, H. *Industrial Archaeology of Dartmoor* David & Charles 1968

Harris, V. *Dartmoor Prison, Past and Present* Brendon & Son c.1875

Haynes, R.G. 'Rabbit Warrens on Dartmoor' *DCNQ* 1986

Haynes, R.G. 'Vermin Traps and Rabbit Warrens on Dartmoor' *Post-Medieval Archaeology* 4. 1970

Hayter-Hames, J. *A History of Chagford* Phillimore & Co Ltd 1981

Hemery, E. *High Dartmoor - Land and People* Robert Hale Ltd 1983

Hemery, E. *Walking Dartmoor's Ancient Tracks* Robert Hale Ltd 1986

Herald Express, various

Hurrell, H.G. *Dartmoor Rabbits* Devon Trust for Nature Conservation 1972

Kelly's Directory of Plymouth and District, various

Linehan, C.D. 'Deserted Sites and Rabbit Warrens on Dartmoor, Devon' *TDA* 1965

Lyall, S. *Dream Cottages* Robert Hale Ltd 1988

Malim, J.W. *The Romance of Dartmoor* C.G. Jowitt 1935

Marshall, W. *Rural Economy of the West of England* 1796

Martin, W.K. *Over the Hills* Michael Joseph Ltd 1968

Michelmore, H.G. *Fishing Facts and Fancies* Wheaton & Co. 1946

Moore, S . & Birkett, P. *A Short History of the Rights of Common Upon the Forest of Dartmoor and the Commons* DPA 1890

O'Hara, Jack *The Dartmoor Foxhounds 1740 - 1985* Privately Published 1985

O'Hara, Jack *The South Devon Hunt* Privately Published 1985

Page, J. Ll. W. *An Exploration of Dartmoor and its Antiquities, with some Account of its Borders* Seeley & Co 1889

Page, J.Ll. W. *The Rivers of Devon from Source to Sea* Seeley & Co 1893

Parsons, Hamlyn 'Papers' Unpublished MS n.d.

Parsons, Hamlyn *Princetown* Privately published 1955

Phillpotts, Eden *The American Prisoner* Methuen & Co Ltd 1904

Risdon, R. *The Chorographical Description or Survey of the County of Devon* Rees & Curtis 1811 (reprint edition)

Robins, J. *Rambling On with John Robins* John Pegg Publishing 1988

Rouse, G.D. *The New Forests of Dartmoor* HMSO 1964

Rowe, J.B. 'Sir Thomas Tyrwhitt and Princetown' *TDA* 37

Scarth-Dixon, William *The South Devon Hunt* The Hunts Association 1923-1924

Stanbrook, E. *Dartmoor - Pictures from the Past - 1* Quay Publications (Brixham) 1987

Stanbrook, E. 'Two French Generals at The Ockery, Princetown', *The Devon Historian* 42: 3-7; 1991

Starkey, F.H. *Odds and Ends from Dartmoor* Privately Published 1984

Tavistock Times, various

Thomson, B. *The Story of Dartmoor Prison* Heineman 1907

Torr, C. *Small Talk at Wreyland* Cambridge Univ. Press 1918-1923

Totnes Times, various

Tozer, E.J.F. *The South Devon Hunt* Privately Published 1916

Transactions of the Devonshire Association, various

Trewman's Exeter Flying Post, various

Vancouver, C. *General View of the Agriculture of the County of Devon, with Observations on the Means of its Improvement* Board of Agriculture 1808

Wade, E.A. *The Redlake Tramway and China Clay Works* Twelveheads Press 1982

Western Antiquary, The, various

Western Morning News, various

White's Directory various

Who's Who in Devonshire 1934 Wilson & Phillips

Worth, R.H. *Worth's Dartmoor* David & Charles 1967 and 1971

INDEX